Searchings in the Silence

George Matheson

Searchings in the Silence

A SERIES OF

Devotional Meditations

BY

REV. GEORGE MATHESON, M.A., D.D., F.R.S.E.

MINISTER OF THE PARISH OF ST. BERNARD'S, EDINBURGH

AUTHOR OF

"*My Aspirations,*" "*Can the Old Faith Live with the New?*" "*Moments on the Mount,*" *&c.*

SECOND EDITION

CASSELL AND COMPANY, LIMITED
LONDON, PARIS & MELBOURNE
1895

PREFACE.

By the title " Searchings in the Silence " I have meant to express the fact that these brief meditations are designed for the stray moments of solitude in which the heart looks in upon itself. No attempt has been made either at uniformity of size or uniformity of manner. I have tried to strike chords of experience, as many and as varied as I have felt within myself. The little book has had long and earnest study. I would like it to be devotional, not by the absence of thought, but by the flashing of suggestion. I would like it to be some small help, not only to the toilers on life's beaten way, but, if possible, even to one or two of that large class who require to preach on the Sundays. If these endeavours have proved a failure, the only excuse which can be pleaded is that the strength of the arm has not been equal to the height of the aim.

G. M.

CONTENTS.

————◦◆◦————

CONTENTS.

CONTENTS.

x CONTENTS.

SEARCHINGS IN THE SILENCE.

A SERIES OF

DEVOTIONAL MEDITATIONS.

———◦◦◦———

I.

Morning Sacrifices.

Psalm v. 3 v.

"My voice shalt Thou hear in the morning, O Lord; in the morning will I direct my prayer unto Thee, and will look up."

WHY "look up"? Is it expectancy — the lifting of the eyes in the hope of an answer? I do not think so. I think it is the looking up not in expectation but in pride — that noble pride which a holy man may feel. The Psalmist says that when he prays he can pray with unabashed countenance — with eyes looking right into the face of God. He has nothing to be ashamed of. He may not gain his desire, but he need not blush for it. And why has he no cause to blush? Because his prayer is offered "in the morning." It is not wrung out by the exigencies of the day. It does not come from the burden and the heat. It is not wakened by the cares of the world. It is not a cry called forth by personal pain. It comes from the heart as yet unburdened, from the spirit as yet free. It mounts by the wings of praise; it soars in the flight of song. It has not been *taught* to fly; it flies by instinct. It turns to the Father as the magnet turns to the pole—not by compulsion but by attraction. It comes before the clouds come, ere ever there is felt a drop of rain. Only the offering of life's morning can say, "I will direct my prayer unto *Thee*."

Oh, Thou whose name is love, it is in the offering of love that Thou rejoicest. There is no sacrifice to Thee like the morning sacrifice. Thou lovest it best because it is the least sacrificial. It is dearest to Thy heart because it is most spontaneous to mine. Thou desirest not sacrifice, oh, my Father. My voice is never so sweet to Thee as when it comes from where the birds sing. The cry of the weary is open to

Thee, but it is not precious to Thee. The prayers of evening can wake Thy pity, but only the prayers of morning can stir Thy joy. Be mine the voice Thou shalt hear in the morning. Many voices cry to Thee from the dusk; let mine be from the dawn. Let me bring Thee my springtime, my freshness, my glory. Let me bring Thee my heart undimmed, my life unweighted. Let me bring Thee a desire for communion that is born not of fear, but of love. Let me pluck for Thee the rose that has not drooped beneath the shower. If my voice shall be heard in the morning, I can lift up my head with joy.

II.

The Illumination of Death.

Matthew iv. 16 v.

" To them which sat in the region and shadow of death light is sprung up."

WHAT a strange antithesis !—" to them which sat in death *light* is sprung up." We should have expected " *life* is sprung up." Is not *life*

the natural contrast to death? Is there any
cure for death but to abolish it? Yes, there is
another cure—to throw light upon it. What
makes death horrible is its darkness. It is not
a thing which I know to be bad; it is a thing
of which by nature I know nothing. What I
want is light. It may be that when the light
comes, I shall find that death needs no trans-
forming. It may be, the sunshine will reveal it
to be already a form of life. I want the
sunshine; I want something to see by, something to judge by, something to read by. I do
not ask that the valley should be made a
mountain; I want light in the valley. Who
can tell but under the shadows of night there
may rest treasures of purest gold. Who can tell
that the valley is not richer than the mountain,
if only the morning were here to disclose its
gems. Truly it was a wonderful insight that
made the prophet say, "to them that sat in
death *light* is sprung up."

Oh, Thou who hast made all things new by
Thy rising sun, I understand death in Thee. I
have called it the great eclipse—and so it is;
but it is the eclipse by *Thee.* It is *Thy*
shadow passing between me and the earth.

Never art Thou so little eclipsed as then. Thou shuttest all the doors that I may speak to Thee alone. Thou drawest the curtains of the eye, Thou hushest the songs of the ear, Thou closest the gates of the past, that I may be alone with Thee. I do not see any change in the shadow, but I have found a new cause for the shadow. I used to think it was an eclipse of *life*—an eclipse of Thee. I thought it was the earth putting out the heaven; I see now it was the heaven putting out the earth. It is not new life but new light that has come. Life was always in the valley, but I mistook its shadow. *Thou* art the shadow of death, oh, my Father; *Thou* art the veil of the temple, Thou art the cloud on the mercy-seat, Thou art the darkness on the cross. I shall not fear any longer to sit in the region of blinding death, since I know that I am blinded by the light above the brightness of the sun.

III.

The Last Survivals of Grief.

Revelation vii. 17 v.

"The Lamb shall lead them unto living fountains of waters; and God shall wipe away all tears from their eyes."

WHAT need that God should wipe away the tears when the Lamb has led to the living waters? Would not joy follow as a matter of course? If my hunger and thirst have been taken away, if my eyes have already rested on the sparkling fountains, surely God need not interpose to dry my tears; will not Nature do that? No. You do not bring back my first joy by restoring my first surroundings. Grief itself robs me of something; it breaks the elastic spring. The child cries after it has ceased to be hurt. The hurt has put it in the valley, and the painlessness cannot at once lift it to the mountain. Some one must put right the spring, must restore the capacity for joy. The fountains in vain will sparkle if the heart has lost its shining.

My God, set right the broken spring; all

my springs are in Thee. Restore to me the *joy* of Thy salvation. Thou hast brought me to Calvary; bring me to Olivet. Thou hast given me back my freedom, give me back my wings. The fountains are nothing without the sense of morning; send me Thy bright and morning star. Forbid the clouds to return to me after the rain is gone. Give me once more not only the old trees of the garden, but the old birds that sang in them. Plant my Eden again in the East—the place of the rising sun. Take away the weariness, the jadedness, the fadedness, that follows the hour of struggle. Heal the shrinking of the sinew that succeeds to the angel's blessing. Remove the paralysis that lingers after the sorrow itself has fled. When I stand beside the fountains of living water, do Thou wipe away past tears from my eyes.

B

IV.

Revelation by Shadow.

Leviticus xvi. 2 v.

"I will appear in the cloud upon the mercy-seat."

APPEAR in a cloud! I thought a cloud was
the place for disappearance; I thought it was
a thing which hid. Yes, in every sphere but
one—the message of mercy. But the pardon
of my God comes to me through pain. I
never know He is near to me till I feel that
He is far away. I never go up to my house
justified till I beat upon my breast and say
"unclean." My sky of conscience does not
begin to clear till its cloud comes; its birds
can only sing in the groaning of my spirit.
It is only when the wind and sea are raging
round my ship that I know the feet of Christ
to be on the waters; the storm of my heart
is wakened by the wings of angels. There is
no darkness on the face of my deep till God
has created the heavens and the earth.

My soul, art thou trembling under thy
cloud? Art thou disturbed by the jarring

chords within thee? Thou need'st not be. Whence hast thou learned the jarring? It can only be from music. Thou hast heard afar off the melodies of Heaven, or thou would'st not quarrel with the sounds of earth. Thou hast gazed on the pure fountains of living water, or thou would'st not murmur at the stagnant pools. Thou has seen the face of the King in His beauty, or thou would'st not shrink from the slave in his deformity. It is thy transfiguration that has made thy cloud. Thy gloom is the child of thy glory, and the shadow that obscures thee is thy God passing by. Oh! mist, clearer than the sunshine; oh! storm, gentler than the lullaby; oh! pain, sweeter than earthly joy — my Father's face appears in thee.

V.

The Impossible Consequence of a Denied Future.

1 Corinthians xv. 13 v.

"But if there be no resurrection of the dead, then is Christ not risen."

"If there be no immortality Christ is dead—the purest, the fairest, the loveliest life that ever breathed has become less than the napkin, less than the grave-clothes, less than the sepulchre." It is to Paul an impossible consequence. He cannot think of Christ as dead. He says "If Christ be dead, death must be a delusion." Did you never feel this experience? You parted with a friend an hour ago, and the next hour you heard that he was dead; you said "impossible!" And when it was confirmed, you said again "impossible! If he be dead, then death is not to die. I must have misnamed it, misread it, mistaken the inscription on its doorway. Death henceforth is a gate of life to me."

Son of Man, whenever I doubt of life, I

think of Thee. Nothing is so impossible as that Thou shouldst be dead. I can imagine the hills to dissolve in vapour, and the stars to melt in smoke, and the rivers to empty themselves in sheer exhaustion; but I feel no limit in Thee. Thou never growest old to me. Last century is old, last year is old, last season is an obsolete fashion; but Thou art not obsolete. Thou art abreast of all the centuries, nay, Thou goest before them like the star. I have never come up with Thee, modern as I am. Thy picture is at home in every land. A thousand have fallen at its side, but it has kept its bloom; old Jerusalem, old Rome, new Rome—it has been young amid them all. Therefore, when oppressed by the sight of death, I shall turn to Thee. I shall see my immortality in Thee. I shall read the possibilities of my soul in Thee. I shall measure the promise of my manhood by Thee. I shall comfort myself by the impossible conclusion "If there be no immortality, Christ is dead."

VI.

Permanent Elation.

Psalm xxviii. 9 v.

" Lift them up for ever."

WHAT a bold aspiration ! To have a perpetual
flow of spirits, to be ever in the air, always
on the wing, invariably above the common
plain—surely it is the wildest dream ! Can any
man reach it ? Has not Peter to dismount
from his air-built tabernacle, and Paul from
his height in the third heaven ? I never get
my exaltation without getting my thorn. Every
mile I soar above the plain is paid for with
depression. Even where I gain the goal, the
goal itself becomes common-place. The star
falls from heaven when I touch it ; the manna
of wonder ceases, and I eat the old corn of
the land. I am the child of reaction ; how dare
I ask to be lifted up for ever ?

Be still, my soul ; thou hast mistaken the
message of thy Father. He does not wish
to lift thee above the plain ; He wants to
lift the plain itself. He would uplift thee as

the Son of Man was lifted up—through the Cross. The joy He seeks for thee is the joy of thy Lord. It is not the elevation of thy heart above its cares; it is the elevation of the cares themselves. He does not promise to arrest depression, but He promises that depression shall not arrest *thee*. He asks thee to believe that even when under the cloud thou art moving still, moving upward, moving onward. "He giveth to His beloved in their sleep"—in their very moments of reaction. The heart cannot beat without its intervening pauses. Thy pauses are thy Father's milestones, oh my soul. They are the times when thou hast ceased to gird thyself, and art carried on a bed; but thou art carried none the less, and carried up the hill. And when thou shalt awake from thy faintness, it shall not be in the spot where thou hast lain down. The moments of seeming waste shall have borne thee leagues aloft. Thou shalt trace thy progress in the tracks thou hast left behind. Thou shalt look out upon the pathway with surprise, and say, "I have been lifted up for ever."

nameless actors

Carried to the gate of our destiny

VII.

Nameless Lives.

Acts iii 2 v.

"And a certain lame man was carried, whom they laid daily at the gate of the temple called Beautiful."

Who carried him? We cannot tell. Peter and John found him at the beautiful gate of the temple, and healed him there. But the main actors of the drama were the men who brought him to the gate, and these are nameless; they are known only to God. Is it not ever so? Have we not all been carried to the gate of our destiny by obscure hands? When we pass through the portals of beauty, do we remember our indebtedness to the unknown? Do we remember the modest lives that, like the angels of Jacob, blessed us and refused to give their names? Do we remember the mothers that planned for us, and the sisters that spun for us, and the strangers by the wayside that lent us a helping hand? How often do I read, "And they brought him to Jesus." Who are "they"? It is known only to God.

They left no personal record ; they planted their flowers and ran away. But the eye of the Master has followed them, and they shall not escape fame ; they have a record in the Book of Life.

Son of Man, gate of all beautiful temples, help me to remember those that carried me to Thee. They sank beneath their burden and made no sign ; they passed and left no monument ; but they opened for me the gate called Beautiful, and I have entered in. The world thinks I have carved my own destiny because my helps are in the mist ; but they are all seen, all sent, by Thee. Forbid that I should be proud of having reached the gate called Beautiful. Let me build on its threshold to the memory of the dead. Let me build to the voices long silent that have led me on. Let me build to the chords of unrecorded hearts. Let me build to the speechless prayers, the unuttered yearnings, the lonely vigils, of hidden lives. Let me build to the unspoken influences that drew my eyes to the morning, and beckoned me up with their song. Thou hast touched my lameness, and set me free ; but the couch that bore my impotence yet lingers at the gate, and, if it would be to me the ivory gate and golden, the relic of my past must enter in.

VIII.

The Disguise of Christ.

Matthew ix. 30 v.

" And their eyes were opened ; and Jesus straitly charged them, saying, See that no man know it."

WHY conceal the miraculous cure ? Because He wanted to be loved, not for His wealth, but for His soul. It is one thing to reveal my wealth after you have loved me ; it is another to tell it beforehand. If you want to prove your boy's love of poetry, don't begin by saying, " this was written by Tennyson." Authority would compel admiration. Conceal the authority ; hide the name ; cut out the title-page ; present the poem as the work of an unnamed hand. And, if the young eye shall kindle spontaneously, if the young heart shall say, " whoever he be, this is a master mind," the altar of art shall be glorified. The Son of Man fears to be first known as the Son of God. He is afraid you judge the work

by its title-page—accept the rhythm for the sake
of the ring. Therefore, He veils Himself; He
enters into a cloud; He puts on the disguise of
a servant; He works wonders by stealth; He
flies from fame; He buries underground the
trophies of His glory. He wants me to love
Him for Himself—through the mean apparel,
through the human weakness, through the common pain. He wants me to find His pearl in
the dust, His beauty in the manger, His crown
in the cross. He wants me to see Him by His
own light—spirit light, soul light. He meets
with me on the road to Emmaus, and talks with
me, and makes my heart burn; but He tells me
not at first that His name is Jesus. Perhaps I
call Him by other names—nature, art, science,
culture, humanity. Be it so; mine eyes are
holden by *His* hand. He covers my face, that I
may not see His glory. He makes me love Him
in disguise. He veils His coronet, that I may
come to His inner beauty. Oh blest disguise!
Oh glorious veil! Oh revealing silence! My
heart finds itself in thee. It has loved a captive,
and he is found to be a king; it has adored a
manger, and it proves to be a palace. I bless His
mighty name that He won my love unknown.

IX.

The Kindness of Love.

1 Corinthians xiii. 4 v.

" Love is kind."

WHAT a small thing to say as an introduction to the praise of love! It is like saying that a great soldier has conquered a mile of ground. Love is so high, and kindness so homely; love, so much in the heavens, and kindness so near the earth. Yes; but the lowliest things are the hardest to illuminate. The triumph of the sun-light is the kindling of the vale. Even so is the triumph of love. It leaps from the mountains to the valleys, and in the valleys it is perfected. Love's morning is in great things, but its evening is in the trifles of life. It rises by shedding its blood, but it culminates by diffusing its kindness. It learns in its dawn how to die, but its fulness tells it how to live. Kindness is the latest flower of love; it is self-surrender in small things. It is the last rose of the heart's summer. It is love playing on the surfaces of life, gilding their very trifles with its glory. It is love become habitual, become chronic, become spontaneous—love running over the borders and making beauty on the dusty way. The keeper of the garden may smile when he can say "love is kind."

Thou Christ of Calvary, give me Thy latest flower. Give me the bloom that runs over the border. Give me the unconscious power of making glad. I have read that after the box was broken its fragrance filled the house. The brokenness was love's morning, but the fragrance was its evening gold. The brokenness was for Thee; the fragrance was for all. I have long had the brokenness, but I have not yet come to the fragrance. My pride has been shattered like the alabaster fragments, and I have lain prostrate at Thy feet; but Martha's part must come after Mary's. Help me into helpfulness; tend me into tenderness; kindle me into kindness. Give me the over-flowing cup—the cup that carries more than myself can hold. Give me the branches running over the wall—making beautiful the hard places. Give me the ministrant hand for Cana, and the beneficent feet for Galilee. Lend me the healing touch which men

call tact, which Thou callest contact—the
power to cure the wound without pressing on
the sore.   Thou shalt perfect Thy loving kindness when Thou hast made my love kind.

X

Ties for the Solitary.

Psalm lxviii. 6 v.

" God setteth the solitary in families."

THERE are some lives to whom the nuptial torch
is denied.   They form no family ties, and, as
the ties into which they were born are
dissolved, one fears that they will be alone.
They need not be.   "God setteth the solitary
in families."   Religion supplies the place of
marriage.   Often have I thought of these words
of the Master, " Whosoever shall do the will of
My Father, which is in heaven, the same is My
brother, and sister, and mother."   The soul
surrendered to God is brother, sister, mother, to
the race of Man.   Who, think you, of merely
human birth, had the widest heart for earthly
ties ?   Was it not the solitary man of Tarsus ?

Who speaks of the family like *him?* Who legislates for the household like him? Who feels for the bereaved like him? And why? Because they who are united to Christ are wedded also to humanity. They have the ring and the robe. They have the bridal garment. They have the marriage supper of the Lamb. They have the cares of all households, the weight of all children, the guidance of all youth, the help of all manhood, the support of all age. It is a crowded life to be married like the *angels*.

Oh Thou who hast consecrated not only the nuptial torch but the want of it, make room for the solitary lives. Make straight not in the desert, but on the highway, a path for those who walk alone. Invite the virgin souls of earth to the marriage supper of the Lamb. Kindle the paternal instinct in the heart that is no father. Light the family altar in the home that has no ties. Fill with the voices of the multitude the spaces left vacant by the brethren. Replenish the isles with Thy fulness—the fulness of human sympathy. Give a crowded interest to spirits outside the crowd. Bring the vision of the city into the silence of the garden. Put the burden of all souls on the life that has no burden. Lay the debt of humanity on those who know not lesser bonds. The isles wait for *Thee* to make them vocal. When Thou hast set the solitary in families there shall be no more sea.

XI

The Light of Life.

Psalm xxxvi. 9 v.

" With Thee is the fountain of life : in Thy light shall we see light."

Do you know the connection between the fulness of life and the vision of brightness? Do you know what it is to have a joy from sheer vitality, to be glad from the very vigour of your strength? It is something like the peace that passeth understanding; it makes one unaccountably happy, unreasonably comfortable. Many a time we laugh when by the standard of the world we ought to cry. The life can often see what the eye cannot see—hope. It is hard to make youth feel impossibility. You may prove to the eye a thousand times that there is no abatement of the flood ; but the heart of vigorous life

shall catch sight of Ararat. The dove of the
spirit brings its olive-branch ere the ark of the
flesh has descried land. Hundreds walk by the
light of life who would fall by the light of facts.
The still, small voice of health within outweighs
all the testimony of the thunder and the earthquake and the fire. In vain shall the tempest
cry to my soul, " Flee as a bird to thy mountain,"
if my soul has said to itself: " Peace, be still."

Son of Man, it is " more life and fuller " that
I want from Thee—not more gardens, not more
sunbeams, not more beauties, but more life.
When my life is low, I see nothing fair; Eden
becomes Gethsemane. My voice Thou canst hear
in the morning, because in the morning my life
is fullest. But at mid-day, when the inner sun
declines, the gates of the New Jerusalem ope for
me in vain; I pass the pearls unseen, I tread the
diamonds unknown. Nothing but blood can save
me from blindness; transfuse Thy blood into my
soul. Give me more nerve, more sinew, more
strength. I ask not new sight; I ask new power
of seeing. The wood is there, and the ram for
the offering is there, if only the inner burning
were there. I need no better revelation; I want
Thy saving health. I want to count the unnoted

c

sunbeams, to mark the unnumbered wells, to record the unacknowledged joys. I want, like Elijah, to see the seven thousand in the place where I thought myself alone, to behold the chariots and horsemen where I knew only the valley of the shadow. There shall be a new heaven and a new earth for me when I have received the light of life.

XII.

A Prayer for Christ.

Luke xxiv. 29 v.

"Abide with us; for it is toward evening and the day is far spent."

WE often use the words as a cry for help in darkness; and they wonderfully express our need. Yet, I think, to the men who first uttered them, they were a prayer for *Christ's* benefit. These men had already reached home; but Christ seemed to be travelling still. They were sorry for Him. The night was dark and the way was long, and they asked Him to come in and rest. Is that a less beautiful prayer? It is ten times more beautiful. To ask my own relief from shadow is human; but to ask Christ's relief from shadow is divine. To bid Him shelter *me* is the cry of my nature; but the offer to shelter *Him* is the voice of God's nature. The climax of all prayer is prayer for the journey of Jesus. Solicitude for *Him*, anxiety for Him, desire for the welfare of Him—this is the summer of supplication. Impotence becomes godlike, helplessness grows heavenly, the bended knee supports the sceptred hand, when I ask "for Jesus' sake."

Oh, Thou, who art still unsheltered in the night of time, abide with me. Come into my poor heart and rest awhile. The wind is cold, and the shades are deep, and the road reveals no end; abide this night with me. In the days of old, didst Thou not strengthen Thyself with love? Didst Thou not climb the lonely height to catch the glimpse of a Father's smile? And shall a brother's smile be powerless? Are there no heights in my heart where Thou canst still repose? My heart burns as Thou talkest; come and warm Thyself at its fire. Too long have I been content to ask *from* Thee; I have learned to ask *for* Thee. I have learned to say before all things, ". Hallowed be *Thy* name, *Thy* kingdom come, Thy will be done in earth as it is in heaven." I would smooth Thy path amid the shadows. I would light Thy way through the gloom. I would ring bells of sympathy across the snow. Above all, I would meet Thee for one hour alone—one hour beneath my roof, one hour within my soul. I would tell Thee before going forth that I at least am with Thee. I would speak a word from my heart into Thy heart, to let Thee feel that it beats with Thine. I would give Thee what strength the little can lend to the great—the response of a kindred spirit, the Amen of a common prayer. Abide with me over this night.

XIII.

The Crown before the Cross.

Hebrews ii. 9 v.

" For the suffering of death crowned with glory and honour."

WHAT a proud provision for so mean an end ! A life crowned for death—surely it is a wasteful thing ! If you knew that your flower must die ere it could reach its summer bloom, would you rear it with a special care ? If you knew that the ship would go down in mid-ocean, would you labour to load it with a freight of precious gold ? No, but this is not a flower; this is not a ship; it is a human soul. The things of nature must weed their thorns to get their crown; but the things of grace get their crown to meet the thorns. The flowers of the soul are planted for the winter. The songs of the night are sent for the night, and they are sent before-hand. God loads with the most precious gold the ship in greatest danger. He sends beauty before the blast, to allay the keenness of the blast. Thy Father seeks not thy pain; He would have sacrifice transmuted into joy. He would warm thee so for the journey as to make thee impervious to cold. He would give thee, ere starting, such a draught of love as should keep thee unsubdued amid the arid sands. The man who would be beautiful in death, must first ascend the summit of Nebo; the crown must precede the cross.

Thou upon whose head were many crowns, give me the crown that came before Thy cross. Send me the flower that preceded Thy thorn and made Thy thorn so bearable. I would rather be crowned with glory *before* the cross, than after it has passed away. It is much to escape, but it is more to conquer; it is good to have joy on Olivet, but it is better to have peace on Calvary. Ennoble me for the hour of sacrifice. Crown me for the altar of duty. Beautify me for the steps of the Dolorous Way. Take me up to Thy transfigured mount ere I suffer, and bathe me in its light unspeakable. Let me sit down at the Passover feast ere I taste the Passover sorrow. Anoint me with the oil of love for every burial of my earthly joy. My cross shall become my crown when Thy crown has preceded my cross.

XIV.

The Voice of God's Silence.

Luke ix. 36 v.

"And when the voice was past, Jesus was found alone."

THERE is a revelation in the silence. There are times when the voice of God dies upon the height, and there is no testimony from the mountain. We call, but it answers not; we question, but there is no reply. Yet there is a substitute; the voice of God is followed by the form of man. I come down from the Divine speculation to the human sympathy. God hides himself that I may see my brother. It is a glorious descent. On the top of the mountain earth seems very small. Its crosses dwindle in the light of eternity. I am in danger of becoming unsympathetic to common pain. The cries of the weary are lost in the songs of the redeemed. Therefore, betimes my Father comes to me in a chariot of silence. He veils Himself from my sight. He shuts the doors of the upper sanctuary. He throws a cloud over the former glory. He forces me to look down instead of up. He leads me from the crown to the cross—from the opened heaven to the imprisoned earth. He shows me Jesus alone—without His retinue, without His pomp, without His kingdom—sinking with pale visage under the weight of human woe. The silence of God reveals Man.

Thou who art beating in vain against the problems of eternity, turn aside and be free. God's silence is a voice. It forbids thee to stand gazing up into heaven. It tells thee that life is not ripe for the tabernacle on the hill. It calls thee back from the mountain to the plain—from the Divine search to the human pity. It puts the veil of Moses on thy face; it teaches thee meekness by the absence of vision. Obey the silence of God. Go down to the Son of Man amid the darkened heavens. Go down to watch with Him in His hour of humiliation. Go down to accompany Him in the agony of man for man. There shall be no loss to thee in the stilling of the Father's voice, if only thereby thou shalt find "Jesus alone."

XV.

The Education for Prayer.

Luke xi. 1 v.

" One of His disciples said, Lord teach us to pray."

You say, " It must have been a very primitive disciple." I do not think so ; I think it must have been St. John. It is, no doubt, a very easy thing to cry, but it is specially difficult to cry for the right thing. No man needs to say, " teach *me* to pray " ; we have all an eye to our own interests. But every man needs to say " teach *us* to pray." What is it that he asks in such a request? It is the abandonment of his whole nature. He says: Teach me to wish nobly, to wish unselfishly, to wish in harmony with others. Teach me to weigh beforehand the force of my own petition. Teach me to ponder whether my personal boon will be the universal joy. What if my desire should be a missile thrown at the common good ! What if the overstrained note of my heart should break the melody of the universe ! What if my prayer should destroy the symmetry of the

house not made with hands! It is an awful
thought and I tremble before it.   I dare not
ask for anything until I have learned to ask in
unison.   I dare not strike the note till my
brother has given me the key.   Until I have
been taught to love, I have not been taught
to pray.

Love on, then, oh my soul.   Prayer is no
lesson for the beginner; it is for the last year.
It is thy mark for the highest prize.   Before it
can be reached by thee, thou must love all
beautiful things—the hallowed name, the coming
Kingdom, the accepted will, the brother's bread,
the forgiven debt, the redeemed evil.   Prayers
are wishes on the wing, and the wish is more
than the wing.   Not the eagle's pinion, but the
eagle's eye, is what thy Father prizes—not thy
rise to God, but what thou seest in God.   It is
easy to fly, but it is hard to fly together.   Thou
must wait for the summer, oh my soul; let not
your flight of prayer be in the winter of self-
love.   Wait for the sight of the common good.
Wait for the sense of a universal care.   Wait for
the impulse of a united life.   Wait for the love
of the loveless, and the sigh for the sighing, and
the pity for the pitiless.   Wait till thou hast

entered into the joy, into the pain, of thy Lord.
In the June of thy spirit thou shalt be taught
to pray.

XVI.

The Burden of Love.

Acts viii. 17 v.

"Then they laid their hands on them, and they received
the Holy Ghost."

"THEY laid their hands on them": there is
a burden imposed in the imparting of every
gift. Each ray of light leaves me less free.
I have to pay for my increase of wealth by
an increase of weightedness. The child is more
joyous than the man, as man counts joy.
The burdens of love are more numerous than
the burdens of law. Love brings me a chain,
albeit it is a golden one. She binds me not
only about the feet of God, but about the
feet of man. I cannot keep my lightness of
heart in the presence of love. The heart which
is full is not light; it reserves its music and
dancing for the prodigal's return. My hour
of revelation is ever my hour of pressure; I

receive God's Spirit by the laying - on of human hands.

Son of Man, I accept the price of Thy revelation; I accept the penalty of love. It was Thine own penalty; love laid on Thee the iniquities of us all. Hadst Thou been less loving, Thou wouldst have suffered less. Had Thy Father not delighted in Thee, He would have delivered Thee; truly Thy cross was Thy crown. If I love like Thee, I must pay for my love like Thee. I must pay for it with heavy-ladenness—with receiving on my head the hands of the multitude. I must be ordained to my ministry, to Thy ministry, by having laid on me the weight of other lives. I wait for Thy ordination. I know its beginning is in pain, but its ending is in peace; the pressure of myriad hands feels at last like the lighting of the dove. Therefore without murmur I lay down the price of loving. I pay the wages of the heart—the penalty of devotion. I bow my head to the burden of human care. I would not be *compelled* to bear Thy cross; I would take it freely, I would choose it in love. Let *me* join the procession along the Dolorous Way. Let *me* get a corner to carry of Thy mighty load. Let me follow, however far off, up the steep of Calvary Let me, at however remote a distance, be a spectator of Thy passion hour. When the multitude have laid their hands upon me, the day of crucifixion shall be the day of love.

XVII.

How to Search for Truth.

1 John i. 5 v.

"God is light."

LIGHT; what is it? It is not something to search for; it is something to search *by*. No man by searching can find out God; but, if he take God without searching, he will find everything else. My evidence for God is what He shews me. I must have a torch to begin with. The room is dark and I have lost something—the key to my own nature. I cannot find it till I have struck a light. There must be light in my hand before I come in—light on the threshold, light at the very door. My progress must not be from the dark into the clear but from the clear into the dark. I must take the wings of the morning ere I set out on my pilgrimage. It is one thing to travel to the uttermost parts of the sea in search of morning; it is another thing to go there on the wings of morning. If there is light beforehand, it will reflect itself upon the sea. The children of the day are those who meet the day before the night. God is His own interpreter; in God's light shall we see light.

My Father, come to me in life's dawn. Help me to find the lost key. All things without Thee are mystery, nay, they are impossible; how shall they prove *Thee* when Thou art needed to prove *them?* The manger will not lead me to the star; but the star can lead me to the manger. If Thou art love, then, Thy best gift must be sacrifice; in that light let me search Thy world. It has pains wrapt up in every pleasure, and who shall explain them? Only Thyself—the Spirit of sacrificial love. We make all things in our own image, and Thou hast made the world in Thine. It is not faultlessly fair; but its spots are from the plan of the Artist.

Let me see the Artist ere I gaze on the picture. Be Thou Thyself my light into every darkness. Go before me into Galilee. Illuminate the mystery of sorrow. Vindicate the rights of pain. Reveal to me that Elijah's chariot must be a fire-chariot. Teach me that the Cross is Divine. Show me that the valley of the shadow belongs to the paths of righteousness. Meet me at the tabernacle door ere I begin the sacrifice. I shall go to life's altar with exceeding joy when Thou shalt send forth Thy light.

XVIII.

The Power of Prophecy

Proverbs xxix. 18 v.

" Where there is no vision the people perish."

THE greatest help to goodness is a bright prospect. The prayer we are all breathing is " Give us this day our bread for to-morrow." We make the child good by promises of the coming gold; but we are all children. The darkest eclipse to any soul is the eclipse of the *approaching* sun. I can stand every present cloud, if only there is a rent prophetic of the blue ; but, where there is no prophecy, I go down the hill.   Often have I thought of these words of the Master, " While the bridegroom *tarried* they all slumbered and slept."   The danger to us all is commonplaceness—the sense that nothing is coming.   The midnight cry is not half so dangerous ; it wakes the pulses of life.   But, to hear no voice at all is an awful thing.   I would rather have the flood without the rainbow than the dry land without the rainbow.   The flood has always its ark ; it braces me for flight, it teaches me to soar. But the level plain with no height to come, the endless road with no goal to gain, the changeless day with no morn to rise—this is my soul's despair.

My Father, open to me the windows of that great deep—to-morrow.   Lend me a ray of the future to light me through the present. I have been told that Thou hast given earth to prepare for heaven ; nay, Thou hast given heaven to prepare for earth.   I have been inverting the order of Thy benefits, oh, my Father.   I have been asking the passing hour to make me ripe for eternity ; it is the vision of eternity that must ripen me for the passing hour. I cannot live a day without Thy morrow; it is from the hills that my aid cometh. I never move freely on the lower plain till I have seen the higher. I need Thy rainbow for the workshop and for the plough. It is when I dream of Thee that I am most practical; it is when I cease to dream of Thee that my task is badly done. Send Thy dream into my day. Send Thy vision of beauty into the workshop of Nazareth. Send Thy light of Bethlehem into the shepherd's fold. Send Thy transfigured glory into the building of my human tabernacles. Let me sweep my earthly room by the light of Thy morning star; I have no patience for man without the vision of Thee.

XIX.

The Comfort of Judgment.

1 Peter iv. 17 v.

"For the time is come that judgment must begin at the house of God."

THERE was a time when men thought very differently. It was once believed that evil fell most heavily on the wrong-doer. That was because the Pure Soul had not yet appeared. When the Pure Soul appeared there came a new revealing; the penalties of life passed me by and fell on *Him.* And, ever since, to those that bear His spirit it has been the same. The thunderbolts of God strike loudest on the good. Conscience makes not cowards of us all; it makes cowards of the whitest. I have read that the dead in Christ rise first to judgment. Why not? The pure mirror is most dimmed by the breath. The good ear is most jarred by the discord. The keen eye is most sensitive to the cloud. The men on the left have no fear of judgment—"When saw we Thee hungry and did not minister unto Thee?" The men

on the right have no salve for a wounded conscience—"When saw we Thee athirst and gave
Thee drink?" Only Christ's Spirit can convince
of sin.

My Father, is the picture of my life worth
Thy criticism? Thy criticism is my conscience.
Do I say "the picture is beautiful"? Then I
am no artist, no member of Thy house, Thy
royal academy. All membership there begins
with judgment. I search my soul for the comfort of pain—the pain of self-condemnation.
How shall I find it? Who shall create within
me the beginning of the art of love? What
shall waken me into discontent with my own
picture? One thing alone, my Father. Let me
gaze on a perfect model. Bring me into Thy
house but for an hour, and point me to the portrait of Jesus. Let me look at the matchless
beauty, at the stainless purity, at the spotless
splendour of the humanly divine. Let me see
the strength in gentleness, the courage in tenderness, the charity in righteousness, that has left
its impress here. Let me catch a glimpse of the
love undying in death, unsinking in the sea,
unconquered in the cross. Then shall I fall
prostrate before Thy judgment seat. Then shall

D 2

my complacency be consumed like filthy rags. I shall call to the rocks to hide me, and to the mountains to cover me from the sight of my own picture. And in the cry I shall find peace—the artist's peace. I shall know by contempt of self that my eyes have rested on the perfect beauty. I shall tell, by the shadow of judgment, that within Thy house I have seen the dawn.

XX.

The Safeguard of Joy.

Luke ii. 10 v.

"Fear not: for, behold, I bring you good tidings of great joy which shall be to all people."

"Good tidings to you which shall be to all." I would fear very much if they were only for me. I would rather have a solitary grief than a solitary joy, oh! my Father. If I must be imprisoned within myself, let it not be by the gates of pearl and gold. My chariot of fire would burn me if I ascended alone. How could I tell my joy to my brother if it were not a universal joy? I can tell my grief to the glad, but not my gladness to the grieving. I dare not spread my banquet at the open window, where the hungry are passing by. Therefore, oh! my Father, I rejoice that Thou hast sent into my heart a ray of glory which is not alone for me. I rejoice that Thou hast given me a treasure which I need not hide from my brother. I rejoice that the light which sparkles in my pool is not from the candle, but from the moon. The candle is for me, but the moon is for all. Put out my candle, oh! my Father. Extinguish the joy that is proud of being unshared. Lower the lamp which shines only on my own mirror. Let down the lights that make a wall between myself and the weary. And over the darkness let there rise the star—Bethlehem's star, humanity's star, the star that shines for one because it shines for all. Let me say: "How glad the shepherds will be, how glad the sages will be, how glad the manger will be!" When I see the common star I shall rejoice with exceeding great joy.

XXI.

The Concealment of Sorrow.

Matthew vi. 17, 18 v.

" But thou, when thou fastest, anoint thine head, and wash thy face; that thou appear not unto men to fast, but unto thy Father which is in secret."

THERE are times when grief itself must be sacrificial—self-concealing. There are seasons in which sorrow has to put on the appearance of brightness. And there is no burden in the world equal to that. It is hard enough to suffer; it is harder still to hide suffering; but it is hardest of all to simulate joy in suffering. To have a smile on the face when there is a tear in the heart, to have a ripple in the voice where there is a deadness in the soul—it requires the highest love. It is something to comfort one who is bearing a burden unshared by you; but to comfort one when you bear the same burden—this is divine. To conceal the breaking of your own heart lest another's heart should break, to keep up under a load lest a brother should be borne

down, to anoint the face in sorrow that a comrade in pain may be relieved—it is to wear the smile of God.

My Father, glorify me with that smile. I am bearing one cross with my brother; let me help him to bear. Let me appear not unto men to fast. Let me give a semblance of lightness to the load. Let me bury my sorrow from the eye that has a common ground for tears. Let me bring grapes of Eshcol, even from the scenes of terror; let me carry the olive-branch from the very waters of the flood. Ere I go out to my afflicted brother I would wash my tears in the fountain of Thy love; I would lay them where those of Magdalene were laid— at the feet of Jesus. I would go into Thy presence-chamber before I enter my house of bereavement; all the plaints of my soul I would unburden to *Thee*. I would leave them there till the evening. I would bury my dead by day in the love of the living; I would let the angel of ministration sit on the stone. I would cover the place of my weeping with the wings of helpfulness; I would deny myself my cross in the presence of Thine. If *Thy* hand shall bury my sorrow, its sepulchre shall be the sepulchre of Moses; no man shall see the spot; it shall appear only to Thee.

XXII.

Work in Grief.

Matthew xvi. 24 v.

"If any man will come after mé, let him take up his cross and follow me."

To take up one's cross and "*follow*" is a very arduous thing. It is easy to take up one's cross and *stand;* easier still to fold it in the arms and lie down; but to carry it about—that is the hard thing. All pain shuns locomotion. It is adverse to collision, adverse to contact, adverse to movement. It craves to nurse its own bitterness; it longs to be alone. Its burden is never so heavy as when the bell rings for daily toil. The waters of Marah seek repose. If I could only *rest* under my cloud I might endure; but the command is too much for me—"Go, work to-day in my vineyard." If I could go without my cross, it would be something; but I cannot. I can no more escape from it than I can escape my own shadow. It clings to me with that attraction which repulsion sometimes gives. It says, " Where thou goest I will go, and where thou lodgest I will lodge." With such a companion I would rather lodge than go; it is hard at once to follow and to bear.

Son of Man, that hardness was Thine. Thine ever was a *carried* cross. Thou never hadst where to lay Thy head in rest. The multitude thronged Thee with their trifling sorrows when a mighty grief was at Thine own door. They complained that the wine had run down in Cana when Thou wert thirsting for a draught of love. They murmured at the scant bread of the wilderness when Thou wert hungering for a human heart. They wept the withering of a slender gourd when Thou wert weeping over the millions of Ninevah. And yet, Thou hadst pity on the gourd. While deep was calling unto deep within Thee, Thou didst not forget the shallow stream. The voice of Thy ocean drowned not the murmur of my brook. My puny cry was overheard by Thy soul in its sorrows, and Thou camest into my world, carrying Thy cross. Let me follow Thee. Let me carry *my* cross into my brother's world. Though it seem a poor grief compared to mine—only a child's cry for the bread that perisheth—give me Thy divine power of locomotion. Help me to empty myself into that which to me is a trifle. Help me to go down from the wilderness into Cana—from my own depths into my brother's shallows. When I have seen them with the microscope of love they shall cease to be shallows; I shall behold them with his weak eyes, I shall magnify them with his weak heart, and, in the power of Thy mighty sympathy, I shall lift my own cross, and come.

XXIII.

The Retarding of God.

Acts iii. 20, 21 v.

" Jesus Christ, whom the heaven must receive until the times of restitution of all things."

Is not this a strange saying—that Christ must become invisible until things are put right? Would we not have expected that God would reveal Himself when things are going wrong? Why should the heaven be silent when the earth is in confusion?—Because discord cannot hear music. The heavens keep many things to them-

Complaining about the Silence of God?

Afresh

selves just because the earth is not prepared for them; if there were more restitution below, there would be less reticence above. Art thou complaining of the silence of God? Lament rather the silence of man. The stars in the Kingdom of thy Father are not seen without the eye of the heart. The voices of the celestial multitude are not heard without the ear of the soul. The touch of the heavenly messengers passing by is not felt without the hand of the Spirit. Why speakest thou of the silence of *God*, when *thine* ear is dull and thine eye is dim and thy hand is blunted? It is thou that imprisonest heaven, not heaven that imprisons thee. Thy Father is retarded in the wings of His love. He calls, but thou hearest not. He beckons, but thou seest not. He touches, but thou art insensible of His pressure. He beats against the bars, but thou deniest him the liberty of the earthly air. He cannot reveal *Himself* till He has restored *thee*.

Restore my soul, oh God! There are green pastures around me for which my eye has no lens, there are quiet waters beside me for which my ear has no chord; restore my soul. There are unknown beauties sleeping in every flower, there are unheard harmonies singing in every breeze;

Restore my Soul O Lord

restore my soul. There are goodness and mercy following me in all valleys, there is a rod and a staff supporting me in all shadows; restore my soul. The path on which I go is already the path of Thy righteousness; open Thou my eyes that I may behold its wonders. The place I call dreadful is even now the house of the Lord; the heavens shall cease to hide Thee when Thou hast restored my soul.

XXIV.

Foresight of Possibilities.

Luke xv. 20 v.

"When he was yet a great way off his father saw him."

It is a divine thing to see merit in advance; only love can do it. It is easy to recognise Moses when he comes down from the splendours of the mount; but to detect him in the ark of bulrushes —that is the hard thing. And every Moses was once in the ark of bulrushes. The mightiest soul that breathes began as a waif on the banks of life's river—a poor, puny, helpless babe. It is only by the faith of others that any of us is hid from the storm—the faith that worketh by love; what eye but this can see the treasures of Egypt through the squalor of the Nile? Therefore it is, that I seek the judgment rather of God than of man. I want to be read by one who can see beneath the facts—who can discern the meridian in the dawn, and the land of promise in the desert sand. I want to be photographed, not as I am, but as I shall be. I want to be taken in the light of to-morrow—in the light of my coming possibilities. I want to have imputed to me the beauty which shall be mine when the day-star shall rise in my heart. Who shall see the rose in the bud? Who shall hear the bells across the snow? Who shall detect the music and dancing in the place where men feed the swine? My brother is too shortsighted for that; I must arise and go to my Father.

Oh, Thou whose infinite love has made Thee infinitely far-seeing, I come to Thee. They tell me that I am saved by my faith; rather it seems to me that I am saved by Thine. It is Thy faith in me, not mine in Thee, that has made me great. I am justified by *Thy* faith, oh! my Father. Behold me in Christ—in the light of the coming day. Look upon me, not as I am,

but as I shall be in the new environment. Listen
to the music of my life, not as it sounds in the
poor, cracked instrument, but as it shall sound
when, with rich stops and intervals, the new
organ comes. Accept the deeds of my body as
they would shine in the resurrection body—with
the taint of corruption expunged, and a stream
of heredity from Thee. View me through the
telescope of love—not as I appear in the distance,
but as I would be when at Thy side. I could
wish no brighter epitaph on my tomb than
this: "When he was yet a great way off,
his Father saw him."

XXV.

The Impersonality of Love.

1 Corinthians xiii. 5 v.

"Love seeketh not her own."

I BELIEVE he means, love averts its eye from
the personal burdens of the heart—crosses the
line of rail that divides my pain from your
pain. Do you know how difficult that is?
Some people seem to think that the mere fact

of pain makes us sympathetic; apart from
Christ, it makes us selfish. If I have one
ailment and you have another, it is very hard
for me to pass from mine to yours. I am
far more apt to say "If I had only your
ailment, it would be nothing; why make *you*
this ado and weep?" There is nothing in
grief which saves from selfishness, any more
than in joy; Christ alone can save. But
Christ can. Love traverses the lines of pain
—passes over from my grief to your grief.
Pride says "My brother deserves to suffer; *I*
had a right to expect better things." But, to
the eye of love, sorrow, when once it comes,
is always sacred. It may have been deserved,
it may have been the wages of sin, it may
have been the child of corruption, before it is
born its parentage may be deprecated; but
the moment it is born it is to Love's eye like
Melchisedek — without father or mother or
descent. It stands for itself alone. It is
reverenced as old age is reverenced—because the
gold has been supplanted by the grey. The
ruins of my wall have come from peace, and
yours from the violence of war; but the ivy
of my heart must cling to yours, and ask not

whence they came. Love, divine love, seeketh not her own.

Jairus, ruler of the synagogue, let me question thee. Art thou murmuring at thy daughter's interrupted cure? The Master was on His way to thy house when He was met by another suppliant. Has God's providence circumvented thee, Jairus? Nay, it has given thee a double blessing. Thy cure is not complete without the interrupting suppliant. The seeming stop was an advance. The halt in the mercy of thy God was a boon to thee. It was a part of thy miracle. It enlarged thy love. It sent thee over thine own wall to the ruined wall of thy neighbour. It told thee thou wert not the only sufferer. It made thy tear trickle to a sister's grave. It lifted thee beyond the sickness of thy house into the sickness of other houses. It took thee out of thine own chariot and put thee in God's chariot of fire, and it brought thee back in the evening—a larger, richer, greater man. Love possesseth more than its own.

XXVI.

The Argument from the Heart.

1 Corinthians xv. 17, 18 v.

"If Christ be not raised, then they also which are fallen asleep in Christ are perished."

"If the highest life be extinguished, what is become of your dead?" It is to me the most unique passage in the Bible. It is the one instance in which the argument for future life is built on the affections of the heart alone. I find it elsewhere on other foundations. I find it built on the life of God. I see it constructed on the needs of conscience. I meet it reared on the ladder of aspiration. But I would have missed something if the words had been unspoken—"If the highest life be extinguished, what is become of your dead?" It would have been the lost chord in the organ of sacred sympathy—the one unappropriated spot in the field where God touches man. I am glad that the chord has not been lost. I am glad that from the sympathetic touch of my God the green spot in my heart

E

is not omitted. I am glad that, amid the
many demands for my future, He allowed one
place to the cry of my love—"If Christ be
not raised, they also that are fallen asleep
have perished."

My soul, be not forgetful of thy human
love. It has its message for eternity. Thy
Father has an argument addressed to thy
heart alone — " If the highest life be extinguished, what is become of your dead? "
He calls thee to Heaven with earthly music;
He appeals to the interest of thy human love.
Would He point thee to that which He knew
to be a shadow? Would He incite thee to
lament the loss of thy earthly love, if He
knew this love to be itself not worth pre-
serving? Why callest thou it earthly? Are
there two kinds of love? Is the water in
the bay diverse from the water of the sea?
Is it not only the sea imprisoned? Thy
heart is but thy Father's love imprisoned—
thy Father's love circumscribed by rocks and
shallows. It has been shut in by the cliffs
of time, and its voice has been reduced to a
murmur. Yet even its murmur has the music
of the everlasting main, and even its broken

strength is mightier than the strength of man. Earth has not made it; earth has *un*-made it, narrowed it. Why should not the loss of earth restore it? Why should not death break the embankment and let love go free? Why should not the murmur rise again into the ocean's tone? Why should not the liberated heart say to the parent sea "I and my Father are one"? Love itself must be dead, if the love of man should perish.

XXVII.

The Hopefulness of St. Paul.

Romans v. 4 v.

"Experience worketh hope."

DOES it? I would have expected Paul to say just the contrary. If this is a world of sin and misery, ought it not to seem blacker as we pass through it? And yet the facts appear to make for Paul. Who are they that take the gloomiest view of life? Is it the aged, the infirm, the wayworn? No; it is the young—the men who are setting out upon their journey. Youth is

E 2

called the age of hope—and so it is ; but it is not
hope for this world.   It is the dream of a fairy
scene far away.   For things as they are, youth
has no mercy; they are too prosaic, too common,
too unclean.   Paul himself was a pessimist in
youth; his hopes were for other worlds than
ours.   To be with Christ was to be "caught up
in the air"—borne beyond the scene.   But, as
the road advanced, the shadows faded.   The
song of the earth-birds became beautiful with
the winding of the way.   The fields of time
grew greener with the westering of life's sun.
The light of Damascus left the air and began to
illuminate the housetops, and the experience
that threatened to work despair became the
parent of hope.

And so, my Father, Thy world is not so bad
a place after all.   It looks gloomier at the enter-
ing, than at the ending, gate.   Thou hast a
special harp for those that have walked upon the
sea.   In the days of my youth I sang to the
scenes of fancy, but my latest harp shall be for
reality.   I shall sing to the praise of the six
days' creation when I have reached the Sabbath.
Put Thy new song in my mouth, oh ! my Father
—the song of Moses and the Lamb, the song of

the desert and the Cross. Reveal to me the gold beneath the dust, the fire within the flint, the flowers around the clay. Reveal to me the beauty of common things, nay, of painful things. Reveal to me the romance of real life, the heroism of daily toil, the power of prosaic sacrifice. Show me the prospect from the west gate of the temple—the gate near to the setting sun. I have looked long enough from the east—the delusive light of morning. I have been seeking a heaven beyond experience, and the chords of my harp have been broken; they shall be strung to a nobler strain when experience itself worketh hope.

XXVIII.

The Will for the Deed.

Ephesians vi. 15 v.

"Your feet shod with the preparation of the gospel of peace."

"Shod with the *preparation* of the gospel," "shod with preparedness to run on the message of peace,"—is that all we should expect from the walk of Christian life? To *prepare* to run seems a small thing. Why does not Paul say that the feet of the soldier of Christ have been hardened by the actual running—strengthened, not by the *preparation*, but by the *proclamation*, of the gospel? Because, if he had said that, he would have cut off the larger part of the army. It is only a limited number of Christ's soldiers who are allowed to serve in the field; the most part have to be content with *readiness* to serve. The souls who do great things in the world are the minority; the mass can only will to do them. I may say, "How beautiful on the mountains are the feet of him that bringeth good tidings," and yet my own feet may be moveless.

I may be forbidden to join the band of active workers. I may be an invalid. I may be weighted with the care of an invalid. I may be struggling with poverty. I may be a victim of nerves. I may be cumbered with much household service. I may be hopelessly commonplace. In all these things my Father says to me "Stay at home." But, spite of all these things, I have the will to go; I would go if these did not forbid me; I do go in spirit every day. I carry messages with the feet of my heart. I am armed with the *preparation* to be a Christian soldier—with the readiness to serve if service were possible. I have given to God my will to give, and He has accepted it as my uniform; He has ordered me a soldier's pay.

Isaac, thou son of Abraham, art thou lamenting the want of thy father's armour? Art thou sighing that, while *he* conquered nations, thou art only permitted to dig wells? Nay, but the sigh is itself a panoply to thee. Thy feet are shod with the preparation, the readiness to go. Thine is the red fire of Mount Moriah, though it is all within. Thine is the resistance unto blood, though the fight is seen by none. Thine is the sacrifice unto death, although thou didst

Readiness
to go

not die.. In thy wells of water God beholds the
possibilities of the deep sea. In thy petty
strifes God hears the roar of the great battle.
In the troubles of thy tiny pool God imputes to
thee the wrestling of the angel. Thy sphere is
narrow but thy heart is wide; stand forth and
take thy crown—the crown of intentions unfulfilled, the prize for mighty deeds designed to
do. Thy monument is side by side with
Abraham's: his has the inscription—"the man
who journeyed"; thine has the tribute of a
larger hope—"the man who was prepared to go."

XXIX.

The God of Jacob.

Psalm xlvi. 7 v.

"The God of Jacob is our refuge."

WHY the God of Jacob? Why not the God of
Abraham, or the God of Isaac? Because Jacob
was the smallest man of the three. He was
the least likely to have a Divine refuge. He
is the type of the largest number—of the most
hopeless number. He is one of the waifs and

strays of nature. He is always doing wrong and running away. He is constantly pulled up from the descent of the precipice. He is pulled up on the hunting-field; he is pulled up at Bethel; he is pulled up at Padan-Aram; he is pulled up at Peniel; he is pulled up even at Goshen, when his love is becoming unjust. A strange man, not all light nor all dark, but living, like his own ladder, between two worlds, and with a touch of both; a man of great aspirings and small fulfilments, dreaming of steps unto heaven, and sleeping on an earthly stair. It is something to know that there is a Divine refuge for such a man; he is so like our common clay, so unheroic, so human. He soars not with Enoch, he floats not with Noah, he mounts not with Moses; he walks upon the rugged earth, and stumbles on the stones. He is one of our own. He belongs to our streets, and lanes, and alleys. He meets us in the wrangling of the mart. He joins us in the burdens of the day. He represents the struggle for existence everywhere. We feel that if there be guidance for him there must be guidance for the million. We say instinctively, "the God of Jacob is *our* refuge."

God of Jacob, I bless Thee for my dreams —my dreams of Thee. It is in my dreams of Thee that Thou art my refuge Often have I wandered through the desert on no other strength than that of the heart's dream. Often, when the way was long and the night was cold. and the pillow was stony, the dream has conquered all. Often hast Thou sent to me a peace that passed understanding. It came where it had no right to come—on the steps of poverty, down the ladder of humiliations. It came when life was low, when fortune was low, when hope was low. It came without a reason—shining by its own light, refusing explanation, defying scrutiny. One moment I had said, "How dreadful is this place!"; and the next I cried, "This is the gate of heaven!" Thou hast followed me with inaudible steps; Thou hast brightened me with invisible sunbeams; Thou hast nourished me with intangible food; Thou hast strengthened me with unaccountable comfort. I have soared without wings; I have sailed without ship; I have climbed, though shrunk in sinew. The man is perfected in weakness whose arms "are made strong by the hand of the mighty God of Jacob."

XXX.

The Wants of Man.

Revelation vii. 16 v.

"They shall hunger no more, neither thirst any more."

MY hope for above is my poverty below. If want be unsatisfied desire, man is the poorest being in the world. He is the only being in the world that has less than he needs. Our Lord says that the other creatures of the earth have *more* than they need. " How many hired servants of my Father have bread and to spare ! " There is a superfluity of riches in the creation below man; it has bread and to spare. Why has the bird such fair plumage, when it has so little sense of beauty ? Why has it so sweet a song, when its ear for music is so low ? Why has it so powerful a wing, when its aspirations are so small ? It is decked with a loveliness it sees not; it is gifted with a melody it hears not; it is endowed with a freedom it appreciates not. It is one of nature's millionaires; its possessions are above its wants. But with thee, my soul, it is otherwise; thy

wants are beyond thy possessions. Thou hast the sense of beauty without the plumage; thou hast the ear for music without the song; thou hast the desire for wings without the power of flight. Thou art not suited to thy surroundings; thou hast a large pitcher and a tiny well. Thy love is long amid the fleeting, broad amid the bounded, high amid the insignificant, deep amid the pools. Thy swallows have no summer, thy larks have no dawn, thy eagles have no firmament, thy doves have no nest. Thou art a voice crying in the wilderness, and thy way is not prepared.

Son of Man, prepare a place for me. There are many mansions in the house of Thy Father, but none has yet taken me in. I am hungry and thirsty, I am homeless and friendless, I am footsore and weary, but no mansion has yet opened for *me*. All other things have places prepared for them—all but my heart. The eye has its light, and the ear has its voices, and the hand has its labours; but my heart has not yet its love. It is powerless, for want of an object; it waits imprisonment to set it free. Prepare a mansion for my heart, Thou whose name is Love. My unplaced heart is the one miracle of creation

—the only thing that violates the law of the Father. Annul the miracle, and give me peace. Give me the harmony with my surroundings that other things enjoy. Break the solitude of my spirit in the universe of life. Find for me a Sabbath of rest amid the mornings and evenings. Build me a tower that shall reach the height of my desires—unto heaven. Send me a promised land, whose reality shall not dim the expectant vision of Moses. At the beautiful gate of Thy temple I shall hunger no more.

XXXI.

The Crucifixion of the Cross.

Revelation vii. 14 v.

"Washed their robes and made them white in the blood of the Lamb."

ROBES that are washed in blood would be expected to come out red; why should the result be so unlike the process?—Because the process of sacrifice which makes me pure must leave no trace of itself. The blood which washes out my stains would, if perpetuated, be itself a stain.

There can be no cross in my completed life. There is a shadow in its dawn, but not in its day. There is a struggle in faith; there is a struggle in hope; but there is no struggle in love. There are some cures which leave a scar; the disease is gone, but the red mark is left which tells of pain. Not all blood washes white. There are struggles in which I conquer, but from which I yet come down with the shrunk sinew; the battle is over, but, even in the daybreak, the wound remains. I have won the fight, but I have lost youth's elastic spring; I halt upon my thigh. But the cross of Christ leaves on me no print of the nails. It heals its own scar. It dries its own blood. It wipes its own tears. It not only redeems, it *restores* my soul. It has no after-effects—no lameness, no sight of men like trees walking. There is no sense of languor, no feeling of soreness, no memory of pain. The cross of yesterday becomes the crown of to-day; the thorn of my winter is made the flower of my spring. The heart's bleeding is staunched when law is one with love.

Son of Man, the shedding of Whose blood ended in perfect peace, let the way of Thy sacrifice be mine. Wash me in Thy blood into

Thy whiteness. Thou hast transformed the red blossom of Calvary into the white bloom of Olivet; make it so also with me. I would not have a thorn in my flesh as the price of my healing. I would not see the bloodstains on the ground when my wound has lost its danger. It is not enough to have my sin crucified; I must have my crucifixion crucified—the red must be washed white. My cross can cleanse my soul; but who shall cleanse my cross? Thou canst, immortal Love. Breathe on me, and my sacrifice shall die. Breathe on me, and I shall receive Thy spirit. Breathe on me, and Thy air shall become my air. It shall no longer stifle me; it shall no more be foreign to me; I shall live in it, move in it, have my being in it. My old law of sacrifice shall become my new life of joy. I shall wear my cross, Thy cross, like a flower; I shall carry Thy burden like a birthright. When I began my journey my garments were dyed with blood; when I reach the heights of Olivet I shall walk in white raiment.

XXXII.

Seeking the Highest.

Matthew xix. 14 v.

" Suffer little children to come unto me."

"SUFFER the lowest to come to the highest";
that is not the world's mode of thinking. The
world thinks we gain most by meeting those on
our own plane. It would send the little ones of
the earth to be judged by the little. It would
bid the incipient artist go to the commonplace
critic. It would tell the fallen soul to repair to
the previously fallen. Not so says Christ. He
says to the labouring and heavy-laden of every
department, "Come unto *Me*"; He says to
those who toil amongst them, "send them to
Me." Ye who have completed your first piece
of workmanship in art or in life, carry it to the
judgment of the highest. Do not go to one a
little above yourselves. He will sneer at your
imperfections. He is too near the line of his
own deliverance. He does not want to be re-
minded of his yesterday. He would fain forget
that he stood lately on the same step of the

stair, and therefore he will disparage the step; he will treat with undue severity your height below himself. But, would you get recognition for the small thing you have, go to the top of the profession. Let your motto be, " I will lift up mine eyes unto the *hills*, whence cometh mine aid." It may seem a bold thing for a sinful man to say "My safety cometh from the Lord, Who made heaven and earth"; but it is not more bold than true. If you would have safety, ignore all steps but the final one. Pass by the converts of last week. Pass the climbers between earth and heaven. Pass the spirits of just men made perfect. Pass the angel and the archangel. Pass the cherubim and seraphim before the throne. Pause not till you reach the throne itself. Enter within the blaze of the burning purity, and spread your workmanship in the light of God. And the fire will not consume it, the light will not wither it, the Master will not despise it. He will see what the intermediate beings cannot see—the oak in the acorn; He will discern in the primal cloud the promise and potency of life. Oh, Magdalene, why standest thou in the house of Simon the leper? Thinkest thou that the leper's own spots will

F

make him mild to yours? They will not; they will intensify his criticism. Come up to the unspotted. Ascend to the stainless. Mount to the highest. Pour not out the treasures of thy repentance at the feet of the half-pure; they will laugh at the ointment of Spikenard, they will scorn the idle tears. Approach the throne, and thou shalt find thy mercy-seat. Come into the sunlight, and thou shalt meet thy dawn. Look up to the hills, and thy valleys shall be illuminated. In the Kingdom of Christ it is the extremes that join together. "Suffer the little ones to come unto Me."

XXXIII.

Christ's Sympathy with Man.

Mark xiv. 28 v.

"I will go before thee into Galilee."

JESUS, Thou art always on before me; nowhere so far in advance as in Galilee. I have never come near to Thee in Galilee— the land of human sorrows, the region of the shadow of death. I am only learning in the

latest times the imitation of Thy work for man.
Thou hast seen further than I into the cause
and into the cure. I had thought that religion
wanted only a soul; Thou hast claimed for
God the redemption of the body. I had
thought that the life of faith demanded the
surrender of earthly comforts; Thou hast
required for that life the restoration of these
comforts. I had thought that the hospital was
for this world, and the Church for the world
to come; Thou hast made the hospital a
temple to the Father's praise. In the culture
of the past Thou art the only modern. None
stood beside Thee in Galilee; Thou troddest
alone the winepress of human pain. None felt
with Thee the sympathy for man as man.
They felt for man as Greek, as Jew, as Roman;
but not as man—not as hopeless, friendless,
landless. It was reserved for *Thee* to lead the
way to Galilee—to the men without a country
and without a home. Thou hast burst all
boundaries but those of sorrow. Thou hast
descended below all accidents—below race, and
clime, and kindred. Thou hast gone down
beneath all qualities—beneath beauty, and
virtue, and fame. Thou hast broken the

F 2

barriers of caste; Thou hast passed the fences
of respectability; Thou hast travelled beyond
the confines of extenuating circumstance. Thou
hast reached the last motive for charity—the
right of hunger to bread. Thou hast invited
man to come to Thee without a plea, nay,
with the very plea of destitution. Thou hast
summoned him in his rags, in his tatters, in
his nothingness: Thou hast accepted him
without merit and without excuse; Thou hast
asked him for no vindication but a cry. We,
of latter days, have claimed the gospel of
charity as our own. We have written an
inscription in golden letters, inviting to our
feast the labouring and heavy-laden. We have
brought it to Galilee with shouts of exultation;
we have called it the symbol of our modern
advancement. But lo! as we have gone to
hang it up on the wall, the wall is already
occupied with another placard, and it is in
words identical with ours. Oh, Son of Man,
Thou hast been before us. Thou hast outrun
our philanthropy; Thou hast anticipated our
benevolence; Thou hast forestalled our charity.
Thou hast modelled our infirmaries; Thou hast
planned our orphanages; Thou hast sketched

our asylums; Thou hast devised our houses of refuge; Thou hast projected our homes of reform. Thou hast vindicated the claims of the returned convict; Thou hast asserted the sacredness of infant life; Thou hast given a hand to the climbing steps of woman. Thou hast outstripped both Peter and John in the race to the ancient sepulchres of humanity; at the end of all our progress we have met Thee in Galilee.

XXXIV.

Asking in Christ's Name.

St. John xvi. 24 v.

" Hitherto have ye asked nothing in my name; ask and ye shall receive."

THE Master is wearying for the development of the pupil. He seeks it in the progress of his prayers. He measures the value of his prayers not by what he wants but by his reason for wanting it. " Ye have asked nothing in my name," means " Ye have asked nothing in my interest." It makes no difference that Adam asks an apple, and John the right hand in the

Developing with Christ

Ask in Christ's interest not ours

Kingdom; they both ask equally amiss, for each desires only his own joy. The fault in Adam is not that he seeks the apple but that he seeks it from the wrong garden. The same fruit may be got from either of two gardens—Eden or Gethsemane. At the gates of Eden I seek it for myself; at the gates of Gethsemane I desire it for another. The one is a request in my own name; the other is in the name of Jesus.

Name above every name, purify my desires. It is by my desires that Thou measurest my progress; teach me to pray. It is not new desires I want; it is a new name in which to bank the old treasures—Thy name instead of mine. Men have called me a worldling in tl e bygone time because I have sought so much for gold. Yet, it is not less of gold I would seek now; it is less of self. I feel as if I needed the wealth of this world more than I ever did; but now I need it for Thee. It is not a change of money; it is a change of investment. I put it in Thy name; I bank it for Thee. I would not have less worldly toil. I would not be seen more seldom in the exchange. I would not relax the wheels of industry nor abate the ardour of enterprise. I want a change of thought, not of theatre. I would send my mérchandise over a mightier sea than ever before it traversed—the ocean of Thy love. I would make the once mammon of unrighteousness a heavenly friend. I would plant schools; I would build colleges; I would raise temples; I would endow hospitals; I would improve the dwellings of the poor; I would supply the destitute with a home; I would provide the fallen with a refuge; I would fill up that which Thou hast left behind. Forbid that I should be too unworldly to pray "Command that these stones be made bread." It was once the tempter's prayer, but Thy Last Supper has made it sacramental. Hitherto I have asked it only for the wants of my own wilderness; when I have heard the cry of the multitude in the desert, I shall breathe it again in *Thy* name.

Ocean of thy love

XXXV.

Charity for Surmounted Things.

Matthew xviii. 10 v.

"Take heed that ye despise not one of these little ones."

It is not broad to despise the narrow. What do I mean by a man of large sympathies? "One who can advance," you say. Yes; but, I think, still more, one who can retreat. It is a very easy thing to extend towards to-morrow; it is a very hard thing to contract towards yesterday. Most of us have an impulse to go on; few of us have a wish to go back. When Paul becomes a man he puts away childish toys; that is natural; that is right; but that is also simple. The arduous thing is to remember that the childish toys are not childish for children—that they are the very poems of the opening years. Do not break the child's image. It is to him no graven image; it stands for a higher likeness than anything in heaven, or earth, or sea. Has he worshipped the golden calf instead of the thunders of Sinai? Yes; but it is not the gold he worships; it is the mystery. The toy was once as mysterious to you as is the thunder now. You wondered what was inside of it; you broke it open to see. Its gold was its mystery; its glory was its unseenness; its brightness was its veil. Judge it not by its discovered delusion. Judge it in the light of those who have not yet broken it open, and found emptiness within. "Take heed that ye despise not one of these little ones."

Christ of love, give me room in my heart for earth's little ones. I have room for the heights, but not the vales, of humanity; let me descend with Thee into the vale. I have been despising those to whom Thou speakest in parables. Remind me that it is *Thou* who speakest in parables—that the crude image covers a faith Divine. Forbid that I should break the image either by logic or laughter. If even Thine angel-reapers feared to pluck up the wheat with the tares, much more may I. I cannot break the casket without destroying the gem. Let me touch the casket tenderly; it is the body of a soul—Thy soul. Let me vaunt not my powers of flight before the face of my walking brother; his walk is, like Enoch's, a walk with Thee. Let me travel by his side along the dusty way.

Let me see with his eyes, feel with his heart, think with his mind. Let me speak to him through his own symbols. Let me appeal to him through his own experience. Let me tell him that beneath the forms his faith and mine are one—the same in substance, equal in power and glory. When I stand on the mount of Thy love, the height shall dissolve the difference between the great and the little ones.

Standing on the mount of God's love

XXXVI.

The Accompaniment of Prayer.

Psalm xlii. 8 v. *(42)*

"In the night his song shall be with me, and my prayer unto the God of my life."

In the night Song and Prayer

"His song and my prayer"—a duet of divine harmony. In every hour of night the two ought to come together; my prayer should accompany God's song. I should not wait for the song to come as an answer to my prayer; I should pray along with the singing. How many acts are helped by simultaneous music. Men march to battle with the strains of melody in their ear. Their march is a great prayer, but it is not enough without the song. I cannot live upon my wants; I cannot even pray upon my wants; I must have hope in order to pray. No man ever cried to his Father who had not in his ear the refrain of an old song. It is by the bow and not by the cloud that I see the exit from the flood. Prayer is the child of expectancy, not of despair. It comes from the smile of God. It rises on the wings of the morning. It is born, not of tears, but of latent joy. It is *in* the night, but not *of* the night; it is in spite of the night. My prayer reposes on the song of God.

Father, sing in my heart that I may pray. I cannot pray till I have heard Thy song. My cry will not come to Thee when I am in the depth of despair; it needs a ray of hope to make it audible. Sing in my heart a song of hope. There are moments in which Thou speakest only in song—songs without words. Such a moment I ask for my prayer. I do not ask a revelation; I do not ask a lifting of the night; I only ask that lightening of the heart which, like the angel of Peniel, refuses to be defined. Music proves nothing; but it helps me to prove all things. Give me Thy music, oh, my Father—the brightness without a reason, the lightness without a cause, the drawing of the curtains where no band is seen. Give me the nameless strength, the indescribable joy, of Jesus—the joy that could subsist through sorrow, the song of the Lamb. There was music in His heart when there was no light for his eye. His was a song without words—without explanation of its being. I ask no more from Thee. Give me but the heart's music in the night, though the night itself be silent—music to pray with, music to march with, music to weep with. I ask no more, but I need no less. Thou hast required the prayer of *faith*; and what is faith but song—a song in the night? Thou hast required the prayer of faith because faith is joy, and joy alone can pray. Night may shew knowledge unto night, but only day can utter speech to day. Let me hear Thy song, and Thou shalt hear my prayer.

XXXVII.

The Practicalness of Christ's Cross.

2 Corinthians iv. 10 v.

" Always bearing about in the body the dying of the Lord Jesus, that the life also of Jesus might be made manifest in our body."

WHAT an unhealthy state of mind! you say— to be ever fondling the idea of death. How can it manifest life to bear death in my body? Will it not sap my energy? Will it not make me a dreamer? Will I not lose all interest in the present world, if I am always thinking of passing from earth to heaven? Yes; but this is no common death of which the apostle speaks; it is the dying of the Lord Jesus. The dying of the Lord Jesus was not the passing from earth to heaven; it was the passing from heaven to earth. Every step of His dying was a step downwards. He took the servant's form. He took the human likeness. He took the fleeting fashion of a man. He took the image of the *humblest* man. He went down deeper than humility. He lost

His personality in love. He became one with the poor, the outcast, the erring. He felt the pains that dwelt in other bodies, the griefs that lived in other souls, the sins that slept in other hearts. At last He touched the lowest ground, and, therefore, the common ground— He completed His dying in the Cross. It was the final stage of His union with man. It brought Him into the heart of the world. It made Him in the deepest sense a citizen of time.

Say not, then, oh, my soul, that to bear Christ's dying within thee is to lose thy hold of earth; it is to double that hold. It is to come from high thought into menial action. It is to empty thyself into the commonplace. It is to descend into what men call reality. It is to leave the green fields of speculation for the thorny paths of practice. It is to give up thy poetry for other people's prose, to resign thy sunlight for thy weak brother's candle. Art thou prepared for this sacrifice, oh, my soul? It wants not less but more love of the world. When Jesus died he went to Galilee. Only in death did He touch the uttermost earth. If thou wouldst bear in thy body His dying, thou must love not death but life. Nothing but the preciousness of life could prompt the dying of the Lord Jesus, or prompt thee to follow that dying. Thou canst not reach it by dreaming; thou must put away thy dream. Thine eye must be fixed on the rude multitude. Thine ear must be caught by the cry of sorrow. Thy hand must be held by the clasp of pain. Thou must dismiss the thought of delectable mountains, or of harps on the glassy sea. Thou must consider the sea that is not glassy, the mountains that are not delectable, the sounds that are not music. Thine must be the love of the prosaic present. If thou wouldst long to depart and be with Christ, it must be, like Him, to get nearer to the earth, closer to the wants of man. To leave the world that is beyond for the world of the passing day—that is the dying of the Lord Jesus.

XXXVIII.

Revelation before Death.

Luke ii. 26 v.

"It was revealed unto him by the Holy Ghost, that he should not see death, before he had seen the Lord's Christ."

WHY should a revelation like this have been such a comfort? Was not death itself to usher in a far greater sight? Was it not like telling a man that he would not see the sun until he had seen a candle? Was not old Simeon on the road to the perfect day— the day of unblemished beauty? How could it add to his bliss to be told that ere he entered the garden he would receive a single rose? Because every scene requires a preliminary revelation. Nothing is beautiful to me unless I recognise it as a memory. Its whole sweetness is its appeal to my past. I only greet with the eye what has once lain near to the *heart.* It would not bring me a step nearer heaven if death were abolished. That which separates me from heaven is not death but life. If I were lifted to God's throne in a chariot of fire, heaven would still be distant from me, unless it were otherwise brought nigh. If I have never held in my arms one treasure of the eternal sea, I may stand on the shore of that sea and feel no thrill. I want the grapes of Eshcol ere I journey to the promised land. Not as a stranger would I go even up the ladder of Jacob. I want the angel to *de*scend before I *a*scend. I want heaven to come to *me* before I go to heaven. I want an olive-branch from the new world to be carried into the Ark while it is yet on the waters, that when I touch the summit of Ararat I may recognise its peace.

Our Father, which art in heaven, reveal Thyself to us ere we are translated to Thee. We have been making too much of the bridge of death. We have said, " first death, and then revelation "; Thou sayest, " first revelation, and then death." Thou wouldst not have us taste of death until we have seen the kingdom of Christ. Let the power of His Resurrection precede the fellowship with His sufferings. Let the vision of Mount Nebo anticipate the promised land. Teach us beforehand the language of the new world. Send us in advance

G

the robes of the upper sanctuary. We would not be unclothed even by death, but only clothed upon. We would have something to carry with us when we leave the sun and moon behind us. We would have a fragment of Thyself in our emptied hand. Give us a gleam of Thy light when the windows of the sense are darkened. Give us a breath of Thy love when the breathing of our hearts is low. Give us a whisper of Thy voice when the voices of earth are faint. Put the child-Christ in the arms of the dying Simeon. Let us come to the tomb through the garden, and forget the fading by reason of the flowers. Let us be led by the hand of life through the valley of the shadow of death. Our departure shall be no severance, if, ere we go, we shall meet with Thee.

XXXIX.

Religious Investments.

Ecclesiastes xi. 1 v.

"Cast thy bread upon the waters; for thou shalt find it after many days."

WHAT a dangerous investment! Was there ever a bank less likely to give safe interest? Yet, in the spiritual world, speculation is the law of God. If I would save my fallen brother, I must give without security. The beggar stands at my door, and says he is starving. Is he starving? What if he be an impostor? What if my gift shall be squandered at the nearest inn? Truly my way to charity is in the sea, and my path through the deep. None the less is it the way, the path, for me. Am I forbidden to say "Let there be light" until the waters be gathered into one place and the dry land appears? How do I know that light itself is not needed to dry the waters? How do I know that my gift may not be the turning-point in the man's life? Does my Father keep His forgiveness until He sees the fruits of the Spirit? No; He says

over the chaos, " Let there be light." He sends
out His sunbeams into the dark. He sends
them out on speculation. He makes an investment of His love in a bank most perilous; He
risks His heart upon the storm. Oh! Love,
divinely speculative, Love that hast not waited
for the assurance of reward, Love that hast
perilled all upon the merest possibility, let me
mould myself in Thee. Many a dove has been
sent from my ark, and has come back no more.
If I listened to the voice of reason, I would say,
" Let me send no further gifts ; they will be lost
on the face of the waters." But Thou, oh Love,
art earlier than reason ; Thou art before all
things. Thou lingerest not for the ceasing of
the storm ; the stillness follows Thee, and does
not precede Thee. Thy smile rises in the
tempest. Thine eye beams in the night. Thy
heart glows in the winter. Thou lightest the
waves while yet they are troubled; Thou givest
in advance Thy gold. Make me in Thine own
image once more. Give me the power to specu-
late—to risk like Thee. Give me the charity
that can live when prophecy has failed and
knowledge ceases—that can believe in the fallen
when there is no sign, and love them when there

is no certainty. The bread I shall cast upon the waters may not be found till after many days; but in the very moment of my casting I shall find *Thee*.

XL.

Unconscious Gifts.

Psalm cxxvii. 2 v.

"He giveth unto His beloved in their sleep."—(R.V.)

THE most beautiful gifts are those of which their possessor is unconscious. God gives to many of us in our waking state, but not to the highest, not to the best beloved. Talent is got by waking, but not genius. Genius is like the nightingale —unconscious of the beauty of its own song. Even so is there a genius of the spirit. There are souls that win their virtue in the school of stern experience ; God gives to them in waking. But there are others, like the garden of Eden, who need not a man to till the ground. They yield their fruit spontaneously. They are beautiful, not because they ought, but because they must. They can no more help being kind than the bee can help making its hive. They are not under the law, but under grace, and so they do everything, not legally, but gracefully. The flowers of their hearts are wild flowers; God alone has tended them; they have bloomed in the light of His smile; they have called no man master. These are they to whom the Father giveth in their sleep.

My Father, give me the blessing of those that "sleep in Jesus." I do not need to die that I may sleep in Jesus; I have but to love. Make me unconscious of myself in the great sleep of love. Take away my sense of merit by removing my sense of struggle. Let me cease to say to myself, "I mean to work for others"; let me work without saying it, without knowing it. Make the doing of good by me an act of genius—a thing of spontaneous beauty. Let me cease to ask myself if I am breathing rightly the air of Thy Spirit; such a question is itself an impeding of the breath. Teach me that the health of Thy countenance is like all health—only known by its loss. I would not purchase its knowledge at such a price. I would be a child in the kingdom of Thy Son—happy, without counting its happiness; guileless, without seeing it is pure. Nay, I would be as Thy Son

Himself—ever on the bosom of the Father in a sleep of self-forgetfulness. None can reveal Thee but those who lie on Thy bosom—who become unconscious of every thought of self. If I would see the King in His beauty, I must lose sight even of my highest grace; Thou givest to Thy beloved only in their sleep.

XLI.

Incompleteness without Christ.

Colossians i. 28 v.

" Perfect in Christ Jesus."

CHRIST is not a miracle; He is that which takes away the miracle. I am a miracle without Him. I am the only unfinished house in the city of God. There is no creature on the earth so great as I; but there is none so unfinished. I am better than the flower of the field and the bird of the air; but I am not nearly so complete. I am less perfect as a man than is the flower as a flower. The flower has no want that is not met by nature; but I have one. If there be no Christ, I have a sense without an object;

unfinished house/body

my want

my faith is vain. I have an object for my eye; I have an object for my ear; I have an object for my hand; but I have no object for my faith. I have the belief in a perfect ideal of beauty; I have a faith that, somehow, somewhere, I shall find it. Has that faith been a dream? Is my life a sunflower without a sun? Is there nothing corresponding to the beauty which I seek? Do I ever find the form than which I can imagine no fairer? I gaze on some favoured spot, and for a moment it seems divine; I shut the eyes, and there rises in fancy a scene more beauteous still. I am unfinished—most unfinished where I am greatest. Nature has left me incomplete. I am a bee without a hive. I build, but there is no edifice; I plan, but there is no order; I paint a picture of beauty, but the original never comes.

Be still, my soul; Nature is not all—not all for *thee*. Thy picture *has* been realised. There has come to thee one exceptional hour which has filled up that which is behind. There has stood before thee a form whose beauty has surpassed thy painting. If thou shouldst close thine eyes a hundred times, thou canst imagine no fairer. He has outstripped fancy; He has outstripped His own star. He has made thee what the flower is, what the bird is—complete. He has given thee what thou hadst not before—a wing for thine own atmosphere. He has made thy promise a fulfilment, thine April a June. He comes not to humiliate thee, but to save thee from humiliation—to break the miracle of thine own unfinishedness. He justifies thee to thyself—justifies thy claim to high predictions, and thy right to noble aims. Nature has broken the pitcher at the fountain; but thou art perfect in Christ Jesus.

XLII.

Perfection not Destructive of Desire.

James i. 4 v.

"Perfect and entire, wanting nothing."

Is that desirable—to lose all *sense* of desire? Is not the cure worse than the disease? How can it be a joy to me to have nothing left to wish for? Nay, but there is no such fear. Perfection is not an absence of desire; it is an absence of want. The satisfaction of a desire

is not its death, but its unimpededness. To fill any craving of my heart is not to remove the craving; it is to remove that which hinders it. Think you that the longing of love is less warm when it has found its object? Not so. The wish of my heart is not killed in being gratified; it lives on in its joy. It is far more apt to be killed by starvation than by fulness. If I want for a long time, the appetite goes; it cannot exist without exercise. Neither can my heart's love; it will die by long denial. To be overflowing, it must be satisfied. Its longing will never be so great as in the moment of realisation. Its hunger will never be so deep as in the hour of repletion. Its craving will never be so strong as in the day of fruition. I shall not cease to desire when I have ceased to be in want. My heart shall rest from its flight; but it shall rest upon its wing.

Son of Man, I do not fear to be made perfect in Thee; I do not fear that when I have gained my promised land I shall weep for my lost wants. The more I possess Thee, the more I must desire Thee. It is the *possession* of Thee that makes me hungry; it is the sight of Thee that makes me athirst. I cry for earthly food before I have tasted it; but I must taste before I can cry for *Thee*. Nothing but the vision of beauty can create my thirst for beauty. It is from the *supply* of my want that my desire comes. My prayer begins, not where Thou art missing, but where Thou art present; it comes from the fulness, and not from the emptiness, of my soul. It is my want that dims my power of wishing, which is my power of prayer. My hope is impeded by fear. My faith is clogged by doubt. My love is blunted by uncertainty. Take away my wants, and Thou shalt perfect my wishes. My hope shall become boundless. My faith shall become cloudless. My love shall become flawless. There shall be no restraint upon the longings of my heart—nothing to say to my wish, " beware what you ask." My desires shall no longer soar in the *night*, but in the day; they shall see where they go, and, therefore, they shall go more buoyantly. I shall seek Thee with a perfect will when I shall want no more.

Struggling
Conscience
Wrestles

XLIII.

The Struggling Conscience.

Genesis xxxii. 24 v.

"There wrestled a man with him until the breaking of the day."

WHEN conscience wrestles with me, it is always in the form of a man. It is my higher self that strives with me—the Christ within. We have all a higher self—a photograph which God took in some pure moment. We have left it behind, but it follows us. It meets us in our silent hours. It confronts us with the spectacle of what we might have been. It refuses to let us go until it has blessed us. It is the same thing as Paul felt when he spoke of the spirit lusting against the flesh. The spirit was his better photograph, his Christ, his hope of glory. It is to all of us our hope of glory. It is not the actual man that makes us feel immortal; it is the ideal man—the man that might have been. That is the reason that to me conscience is precious even when it wounds. It is no foreign hand that strikes

me; it is my higher self, my inner man, my
likeness as God sees it. It is the image of
me that is hung up in heaven—the picture on
which my Father gazes to avert despair. It
is not only with *me* that the man wrestles; he
wrestles with the Father *for* me. He pleads
my future possibilities. He suggests my coming
glory. He tells what I would be in less vile
raiment. He shows what I *may* be with the
ring and the robe. He reveals how I shall
look at the breaking of the day.

My Father, behold me in Thy Son. Let
the Divine Man wrestle for me in Thy heart.
See in Him my shield; look on the face of
Thine anointed. When Thy heart is grieved
for me, turn to the Man on Thy right hand.
He is my true self—Thine *ideal* of myself.
He is the likeness of what I shall be at daybreak; keep Thine eye on my daybreak, oh!
my God. Let the sight of Him be my hiding-
place from the storm, and my covert from the
tempest; it will avert the tempest of Thy
sorrow. In the hour of evil, a man cries in
my heart, "thou shalt not"; let His cry
answer for me. Impute to me the inner Christ,
the better self. The groanings of my spirit

are the voice of Thy Spirit; let them intercede for me. Judge me by the Man whom Thou hast ordained—the wrestling man. Judge me by the high resolve, the lofty aim, the kindling thought. Judge me by the eager wish whose flight the flesh cannot follow, by the strong will whose stroke the hand cannot second. Judge me by the pain that succeeds to failure, the wound that comes from sinning, the remorse that waits on doing wrong. Judge me, not by the breaking of the mirror, but by the sight of the face I have seen in breaking it; for the face is the higher man—the Man Christ Jesus.

XLIV.

The Temptation to Silence Conscience.

Genesis xxxii. 26 v.

"And he said, Let me go, for the day breaketh."

IT is at daybreak that our angels flee away. The struggles of conscience are most felt at night. In the silent hour, when the day has gone to rest, and the pulse of the great city lies still, my heart wakes to its own significance;

I realise what an awful thing it is to be a human soul. But when the morning comes, I lose my sense of importance, and, with it, my feeling of solemnity. I cease to be a solitary man—an island of life in the darkness. I cling to the visible garment of the outer universe. I become one of the vast multitude. I lose my separate conscience, and, along with it, my separate struggle. The angel that wrestled with me when alone, deserts me in the crowd. The vows of night are cancelled by the rising sun. The songs of night are drowned by the wheels of merchandise. The prayers of nigh are ended with the breaking of the day.

My Father, help me to retain my night-angel. May I refuse to let him go till he has blessed me for the day. Teach me that the struggles of my angel, though they come by night, are not meant for night. Why should he leave me with the light of morning? Is there more of earth in the morning than in the night? Then, I need him more, I need *Thee* more, oh, my Father. It is for moments most unlike Thee that I most require Thee. It is easy to feel Thy presence in the void—in the solitude of night, where no other presence comes. But to feel Thee where there is no void, to perceive Thee in the heart of other things, to behold Thee among the forms which men call common and unclean—this is indeed to be religious. It is easy to know Thy face when I see nothing between me and the stars. But when, like Peter, I see let down from heaven a great sheet filled with prosaic fare, it is hard to believe that it comes from Thee. It is easy to recognise Thee when I am on the wing; it is hard to feel Thy presence when I halt upon my thigh. It is for the noontide that I need Thee, oh, my Father. Leave me not when the romance of life leaves me. Leave me not when the solemn stars have faded into the light of common day. Leave me not when the gate of the temple called Beautiful has closed, and I stand with lame feet upon the dusty way. Thou hast followed me into the silence, and I shall follow Thee into the crowd; I will not part with Thee at the breaking of the day.

XLV.

The Enlargement of the Soul.

2 Corinthians vi. 13 v.

" Be ye also enlarged."

How shall I enlarge my *heart?* When I want to enlarge my *field*, I know what to do; I break down the fences that mark it off from other fields. But the evil of my natural heart is that it has already too few fences—too much of its own ground. If I would enlarge my heart, I must do it in the opposite way from the field. I must curtail my own extent by giving more space to the fields of others; I must put up new fences, to shut out my self-nature. The enlargement of my heart is love, and love is a limiting of myself. It is a setting up of other kingdoms within my own domains. Love takes the half of my field and gives it to my brother, and then against myself it writes over it the words, " no trespassing." The enlargement of my heart is the death of selfish freedom—the death which Paul says " is gain." It is the captivity to Christ, yea, the

captivity *of* Christ.   Often have I thought of
these words, "He saved others; Himself He
cannot save."   They were meant for a reproach,
but they were the grandest compliment ever
paid to love.   It is the glory of love that it
can say, "I cannot."   It is the glory of love
that it can empty itself into a servant's form,
and be compelled by its own nature to obey.
It is the glory of love that it "constraineth
us," forceth us, maketh prisoners of us.   It is
the glory of love that it has a crown of thorns
—thorns of sympathetic pain, which it is powerless to escape, and bound to bear.   It is the
crown for which Jesus prayed when He said,
"Glorify Thy Son."

Son of Man, who hast reached Thy highest
glory in the inability to save Thyself, grant
me this enlarging powerlessness.   Raise up in
my heart that Divine barrier called Love.   Shut
the door upon my selfish nature.   Put a wall
of compassion in the middle of my soul.   Make
it impossible for me to hurt my brother, to
trespass on the ground of my brother.   Nay,
that is a small thing; make it essential for me
to enter the service of my brother, to become a
worker in his field.   My heart is not free until

it is imprisoned; it only says " I can " when it says " I must." Put Thy gold fetters on it, that it may expand. Bring it down from the wing into the cage, that it may have room to grow. Take away its freedom of indifference. Make it the slave of something, of somebody. Give it an aim to live for, to die for. Give it a yoke to bear, that it may find rest. Enclose it in human bonds, that it may learn to throb. When the bars of Thy love shall encircle it, it shall be enlarged indeed.

XLVI.

Why God Hides Himself.

Habakkuk iii. 4 v.

" There was the hiding of his power."

My Father pretends to be not omnipotent. It is the most beautiful fiction in all the world. It gives me what I call the freedom of the will. He puts me on an open plain, and tells me to walk alone. He never really lets me go, never loses hold of the fringe of my garment; but He hides the guidance of His hand, and

H 2

makes it appear as if He were not there. He
stands at a seeming distance, and says "Come."
He makes me think that I am all by myself.
He does not let me see His everlasting arms
around me. He does not let me feel the
encircling care lest I dash my foot against a
stone. He does not let me know that I am
guarded utterly, jealously, all round. He
conceals His supporting arm in a mist; He
leaves a margin for my own choice. If I
need the fire by night, I need still more the
cloud by day. So much vision would destroy
my manhood; it would *compel* me to come in.
I must not be compelled to come in; I must
come of my own accord. I must not be driven
from forbidden fruit by the flaming sword and
the cherubim. The stars are so driven; there is
compulsion into the way of light. But into
the way of life there is no compulsion. I am
not a star; I am a soul. I may not be driven;
I must choose. God must hide himself amid
the trees of the garden that I may feel myself
to be free.

Therefore, I am glad, oh, my Father, that
Thou hast not wholly revealed Thyself; I am
glad there is a cloud as well as a bow. Men

praise Thee for Thy many voices; they ought
to praise Thee for Thy silence too.   Thy silence
is precious to me; it gives a voice to my heart.
In Thy silence my heart finds room; faith
soars, imagination speeds, hope beckons, will
longs, conscience cries.   Thy silence is my
music; Thy shadow is my revealing; Thy
night is my day.   When I see not Thy hand
of retribution, I awake to the majesty of un-
aided virtue.   When I hear not the sound of
Thy last trumpet, I listen to the judgment
of the still, small voice.   When I read not
Thy writing on the wall, I consult the tables
of my own book of life.   The ceasing of the
thunders of Sinai has left room for the sighing
of my love; I am glad that Thou hast hid
the fulness of Thy power.

XLVII.

Man Revealed to Himself.

1 Corinthians xiv. 25 v.

" And thus are the secrets of his heart made manifest."

MADE manifest to whom? Not to others, but to the man himself. Nothing hides a secret from me like my own heart. I know more of my friend than I do of myself. Truly was it said that the heart is deceitful above all things. It keeps a secret drawer which itself cannot open. There are no surprises like the surprises of my own soul at news of itself. There are treasures lying latent in my heart, of whose possibility I do not dream. I never *can* dream of my own riches until I am touched by a kindred soul. Till the kindred soul appears, my sleep is unbroken. But with the sight of that other face, the spell vanishes; I first dream, then wake. I am like a deaf-mute restored to hearing. I find that the blank space was a foaming cataract waiting for the unsealing of the waters. The silence was peopled with imprisoned passions. There were tempests of love longing to be uttered, floods of emotion ready to be poured, torrents of tenderness eager to flow. They waited for the angel to roll away the stone, and then they revealed themselves—revealed within the sepulchre a living man.

Thou Light and Life of men, to Whom the secrets of all hearts are open, my heart is a sepulchre until it finds Thee. It is not to know my future that I most need to find Thee; it is to know my present. When I meet Thee, I discover *myself.* The books of my life are never really opened till I see *Thee* on the throne. Thou art to me what the light is to my picture on the wall. It has hung for long hours in a dark room, and I myself did not see it. But the breaking of Thy day has fallen upon my picture, and, for the first time, I have beheld myself. And, now that I behold myself, I know that all along, I have been in search of *Thee.* I did not see Thee when I was under the fig-tree; but now that Thou hast shaken the leaves, I know that I was waiting for *Thee.* I know it because Thou art not wholly new to me. I seem to have heard Thy voice before. It comes to me like a refrain, like a memory. It wakes echoes in my past; it makes me say, "When did I hear that song?" Thou hast swept the chords of my harp, and revealed its music. Thou hast touched the strings of my love and evoked its passion. Thou hast lighted the room of my conscience, and displayed its ideal portrait; and lo! it is the likeness of Thyself. The secrets of my heart are made manifest in Thee.

XLVIII.

Provision in Advance.

John x. 3 v.

"To him the porter openeth."

WHEN a man approaches the right door, he does not need to open it himself; it is done for him. There is always someone behind the right door ready to let me in. I may knock for ages at the wrong one; I may beat with clubs of iron against opposing gates; if they are not the gates for me, they will not yield. But when I come to the true gate, the porter opens it in advance. I never require to knock; the barriers recede from before me. I do not carve my openings in life; they are made before I come up—made by what men call accident. Pharaoh's daughter would have walked by the banks of the Nile though I had not been drowning. The ram would have been caught in the thicket though I had never climbed the steep of Moriah. The door that lets me in may have opened to let another out. "Then, it all happened quite naturally," you say; "there was no Providence in it." Yes, it all happened quite naturally, and, therefore, there *was* a Providence in it. What is Providence? It is the weaving of my life into another life; it is the music of footsteps moving different ways. The shepherds come to watch, and the angels come to sing; but the watchers and the singers meet face to face, and each enters by the other's door.

I thank Thee, oh, my Father, that the doors of my life are not left to be opened by me. I thank Thee that behind the right door the porter ever stands. Thou hast set before me, not a door to be opened, but "an open door." When I come up, I shall find it already ajar, and I shall enter easily in. It is the *distance* that appals me. My door seems a closed one till I reach it. The struggles of my heart are struggles of anticipation. I need faith, not for the moment, but for the prospect. When the door is distant, the opening is invisible. Be it so, my Father; Thou hast promised me my bread for each day, but not my bread for to-morrow. Yet, let me believe that to-morrow's door has been opened to-day. Let me believe that, while I was yet afar off, my Father saw me. Let me believe that the Ararat of my peace was prepared below the flood. Teach me that the fulness of my time is not my struggle, but my facility. Teach me that, if my hour were come, the water would become wine spontaneously. Teach me that, if the door has opened to the instinct of the bee, it must have opened still wider to my soul. I have lost a sense in becoming man. Give me the bee's unconsciousness of self, that I may be filled with Thy Divine instinct, and led without struggle to the ivory gate and golden. I shall know the true door by one direction; it is the door that is already open.

XLIX.

Instinctive Christians.

2 Peter iii. 14 v.

"That ye may be found of Him in peace."

THERE are two sets of minds in the Christian life—those who find Christ, and those whom Christ finds. Those who find Christ are active; those who are found by Christ are passive. The one have a hard struggle; the other enter the gates "in peace." There are some whose experience is that of the wise men of the east; they search for the star, and discover it after many days. There are others like the keepers of the flock of Bethlehem; they are engaged in their own work, and the star comes to *them*. The men of the east are men of talent; they plan, and they succeed. But the keepers of the flock are men of genius; they never need to plan; they are illuminated in a moment. In the midst of their daily toil there is suddenly with them a multitude of the heavenly host singing "glory." They are like the great masters in music; their work costs them little trouble. They are born to love; they are made to sacrifice; they are bound to say the right thing at the right time. The garment of goodness becomes them, sits gracefully on them. It is a garment, not of heaviness, but of praise. The men who are found by Christ take the kingdom by violence.

Son of Man, I would like to be one of Thy men of genius—one of those who are *found* by Thee. I would like Thy life to be my starting-point rather than my goal. I would rather fly *with* Thee than *to* Thee. I do not want to wait for Thy rest till the end of the journey; I want to journey on Thy wing. I would have rest before I start—rest to help my start, rest to sustain my start. It is by Thy rest I would travel; I would walk by rest, run by rest, fly by rest. If I come first to seek Thee, I shall be weary when I find Thee; however short the way, it is too long without Thee. Shall I ask the wings of a dove, that I may fly away and be at rest? Nay; let me get Thy rest, and then I shall have the wings. There is no power of motion like the repose in Thee. The brooding of Thy Spirit is a rushing, mighty wind; it will carry me beyond myself—into the life of my brother. Come, then, to me, oh, Dove of the Firmament. Wait not till I seek Thee, amid the troubles of the wilderness. Descend upon me at the dawn. Light upon me when the heavens are opened, and the waters of youth are sparkling. Abide on me when it is morning and the day is yet to begin. Spread Thy wings over me before I go out into the temptation. Bring Thy message of peace, and I shall be strengthened for every war. I shall find myself when I am found by Thee.

———————

L

The Retrieving of Yesterday.

Isaiah ix. 3 v.

"They joy before Thee according to the joy in harvest."

THE kind of joy which I would like to have in the presence of God is the joy of harvest. What is the joy of harvest? It is a resurrection joy. It is not the gladness which comes from getting anything new; it is the satisfaction of seeing the rising of buried things—the bursting from the ground of what I believed to be dead.

There is no joy to me like that. It is far more than being lifted out of my trouble; it is the lifting of my trouble itself. It is good to be taken from the fearful pit, and from the miry clay; but it is not the highest thing. The highest thing is to find that the miry clay itself contained gems of gold. It is much to be delivered from my past; but it is more to have my past vindicated, justified—to be able to say, "It was good for me to have been afflicted." I do not think that Job's was a perfect compensation. He was cured of his ailments, and he received new houses and lands. It was a joy, but it was not a harvest joy. It did not explain the years of famine. It did not make up for the time of waste. It did not say why the night had been. You may tell me that the night is far spent, and the day is at hand; it is well, but it is not sufficient. I want to know that there are songs in the night itself. I want to feel that I have not been wasting time. I want to believe that even my desert moments have been a march to the promised land. I would have the joy of reaping the buried grain —the joy of harvest.

Oh! Thou, who art come to seek and to save

lost things, buried things, I lift mine eyes to
Thee. Many have offered me a golden morrow;
Thou alone hast offered to retrieve my yesterday.
Many would give me a new garden; Thou alone
rememberest the treasure hid in the old ground.
Give me back my past, oh, Lord. Restore to me
the waste places of my heart. Reveal to me the
meaning of my failures. Teach me the track of
the path I deemed trackless. Show me the
angel sitting on the tomb of my buried self.
Show me that the man with whom I wrestled
at Peniel was a man from heaven. Show me
the vision of beauty that hovered over my pillow
of stone. Show me that there was manna in my
desert, which even Canaan did not hold. Then
shall mine be a harvest joy, a resurrection joy,
the joy of gathering the buried past. Then
shall my heart be satisfied that the travail of
the soul was autumn's gain. Then shall my
mountain view indeed be beautiful, for it shall
be seen from the place of my former valley.
The joy of harvest is the joy of redeeming
love.

LI.

The Blessing of Conflict.

Psalm lxxviii. 5 v.

" For He established a testimony in Jacob . . . . . .
which He commanded our fathers that they should make
them known to their children."

WHAT is the testimony of Jacob? It is his
witness to the power of sorrow. His whole
life is such a witness. He lies at night on a
couch of stone, bemoaning his hard lot; and
he has such a dream as never came from bed
of down. He wrestles amid the shadows with
a great calamity; and, when the day breaks, lo!
it is an angel. He gets a bodily imperfection,
in the shape of a shrunk sinew. He fears it
will lower his influence among a sensuous race.
And, behold! it heightens it—heightens it so
much that men call him by a new name—Israel,
the Prince of God. That is the testimony of
Jacob; that is the testimony which the Psalmist
bids us spread from sire to son. Tell your
children, he says, that the new name, reached
by struggle, is the law of all life. Tell them,

The blessing of conflict

Jacob's testimony to the power of sorrow

Jacob's new name Israel — Prince of God

couch of stone

Bodily imperfection shrunk sinew

New name reach by struggle is the law of life

on the very threshold of the dawn, that the experience of Jacob is to be *their* experience. Tell them to include in their dream of life the couch of stone, to find a place for the daybreak in the midnight struggle, to see the mercy of God in the impotent limb. Tell them that if they would ascend to heaven, it must be "on stepping-stones of their dead selves," for the ladder will not bear the weight of a selfish heart, and the gold of the New Jerusalem is only seen by averted eyes.

Son of Man, teach me what it is to be made for *Thee*. I have begun life with the vision of Jacob's dream, but without the vision of Jacob's couch; I have seen the shining, but not the shade. Reveal to me that what I call the shade, Thou callest the shining. Reveal to me that the night in my hemisphere is the day in Thine. Reveal to me that the strait gate and the narrow way must needs be the gate to glory. I used to think my sacrifices were sent to prepare me for heaven by contrast; tell me it is not so. Let me see that the gate to heaven is sacrifice, because heaven itself is sacrifice. Teach me the harmony between the way, the truth, and the life. Show me the symmetry between Thy

I

Cross and Thy Crown. Let me learn that the divineness of love means the divineness of pain. Let me learn that eternal life is the power of perpetually dying. Let me learn that the flowers of Paradise are the blossoms of early tears—the daybreak vision of what was sewn by night. So shall I hear the testimony of Jacob.

LII.

The Power of Prospect.

2 Samuel xxii. 13 v.

" Through the brightness before Him were coals of fire kindled."

THERE are two kinds of brightness—memory and hope. Memory is the glass of old age; it is the brightness behind. Hope is the glass of youth; it is the brightness before. Memory sees a glorified past, with its clouds transmuted into gold; hope beholds a radiant future, with no clouds to be transmuted. Memory is beautiful, but it is not kindling; it stirs not the fire of enthusiasm; the vision of a brightness behind me is allied to tears. But hope makes me glow.

Symmetry between cross and crown

Learn to perpetually live must perpetually die now

Memory glass of old age of glorified past

Two kinds of brightness. Memory and hope.

Hope: glass of youth beholds radiant future, expectation hope

The vision of to-morrow fires me. It is not brighter than yesterday; but yesterday is past, and this is coming. The record of the past can make me grateful, but only the sight of the future can make me strong; in "the brightness before" are coals of fire kindled.

My Father, give me back my youth. Give me back that glow of expectation which lived in to-morrow, and had no yesterday. Give me back the glass of hope which swept the coming horizon and saw no cloud therein. Give me back the sight of the jasper sea, and the view of the emerald rainbow, and the glimpse of a world without night. Let Thy Christ make me a child again—a child on fire with promises. If *His* flame shall kindle my bush, no earthly care shall consume it. The plagues of Egypt will not; the waters of Marah will not; the thunders of Sinai will not; the dearth of the desert will not; the sunset of Nebo will not. If the Promised Land be before me, clouds and darkness shall in vain be round about me; their elements shall melt with fervent heat in the brightness of hope's glory.

LIII.

The Power of God's Presence.

Isaiah lxiii. 9 v.

"The angel of His presence saved them."

STRANGE that men should be saved by a presence;
it is such a quiet thing. Salvation might be
thought to require something strong, potent,
compelling; we are surprised at an influence so
gentle. Yet, I think, the most potent thing in
the world is just a presence. What is it that
determines the rank in society? It is the
answer to the question, "Who are *there?*"
What is it that brings condolence to an hour of
bereavement? It is just the saying of one to
another, "I am with you." It is not what is
spoken; it is not what is done; it is the sense
that some one is there. So is it with my Father.
I am not anxious to know the *why*, but only the
where, of God. It matters little to me for what
purpose He walks upon the storm, nor is it of
deadly consequence whether or not He shall say,
"Peace, be still." The all-important thing is
that the feet upon the sea should be His feet—

P. 132-4 Searchings in the silence

er's. Tell me that, and I ask is all the difference in the ent room and an empty room. nionship where there is no written, " In Thy *presence* is In the very sense that my Father is there, though He speak not, though He whisper not, though He write not His message in a book, there comes to my heart a great calm.

Reveal Thy presence, oh, my God. I want Thy presence even more than Thy power. The stilling of the waves is something; but it is not the main thing. The main thing is that Thy way is *in* the sea and Thy path *through* the deep. I would rather have the bow in the cloud than the cloudlessness without the bow. I would rather have the storm with Thee than the calm without the sign of Thee. I would rather have the cross with Thy presence than the crown in Thine absence. Art Thou in the thunder, and the earthquake, and the fire? That is all I want to know. I ask not the revealing of Thy truth; I ask the revealing of Thee. Keep Thy mysteries in the great deep; bury Thy purposes in the vast silence; conceal, if Thou wilt, the meaning of my terrors and my tears; but tell me—oh! tell me, that the room which is silent is not empty. Tell me that in the midst of the furnace is one like unto the Son of Man. Tell me that amid the lightnings of Mount Sinai sits the form of the Law-giver. Tell me that the burning bush of Horeb was lit by the torch of love. I am not afraid of any judgment-day where *Thou* art on the throne; the angel of Thy presence is enough for me.

LIV

Looking Through the Crystal.

Revelation xxii. 1 v.

"And he shewed me a pure river of water of life, clear as crystal, proceeding out of the throne of God and of the Lamb."

It is a clearness of *revelation* that is here spoken of. The crystal is an emblem of revelation. Men have looked into it to know the future. What St. John wants to know is the present. His mystery is not heaven, but earth; it is Patmos, with its separating sea. The revelation

he wants is an unfolding of the secret of
sorrow. And where does he find this crystal
river of revealing? Strangely enough, in God.
We are often apt to explain why there should
be a mystery in sorrow by saying that God's
ways are above us. St. John says it is only
by looking at God's ways that the mystery of
sorrow vanishes. It is "from the throne of God
and of the Lamb" that the river of revelation
flows. "The throne of God and the Lamb"—
what is that? It is the power of sacrifice.
The plan of the world is as clear as crystal
when I see the Lamb on the throne. As long
as I think sacrifice a blemish, nothing can
explain it. If heaven is incompatible with
pain, the crystal can never be clear. But if
pain be on the throne of God, if sorrow be
a necessity of love divine, my view is luminous.
If the river that makes glad comes from the
fountain of sacrifice, if the pleasures at God's
right hand are born of self-surrender, I can
see with satisfaction the travail of my soul.
I may well drink of the river of *His* pleasures.

My Father, let me see the *source* of Thy
stream. I am not afraid of anything that it
has carried from the beginning. When I first

saw the dark places in the river, I thought
they had come in somewhere during its course.
But if I am told that they are there from
the days of the *stream*, it makes all the difference. Nothing impure can come from *Thee*.
The source of the stream is Thy Throne. If
sacrifice be on Thy Throne, the winter is past.
I am not anxious to trace the river forward to
its ocean ; I would rather trace it backward
to its rise. They tell me that my pain will
issue in glory; but has it issued *from* glory—
from Thee ? Reveal Thy Christ, oh, God !
Reveal the divinity of sacrifice. Reveal that
the Lamb was slain from the foundation. Reveal
that not Eden, but Gethsemane, was the world's
garden. Reveal that the red, and not the white,
blossom was the goal in Thy heart which made
the dawn in my life. The veil of my temple is
not sorrow, but its seeming accidentalness ; rend
Thou my temple-veil. I shall have a front
view of the universe when I see the Lamb on
the Throne.

LV.

Light in Christ.

John i. 4 v.

"The life was the light of men."

CHRIST has illuminated the world, not by what
He did, but by what He was; His *life* is the
Light of Men. We speak of a man's life-work;
the work of Jesus was His life itself. When I
want to get light from others, I consult their
books; when I want to get light from Christ, I
hang up His picture. It is not what He says
that I chiefly treasure. The Sermon on the
Mount is grand; but the Preacher is greater.
It is good to be told that the pure in heart shall
see God; but the vision of heaven in a pure
man's face outweighs it all. They tell us that
the Easter morning has revealed His glory;
rather would I say that His glory has revealed
the Easter morning. It is not resurrection that
has made Christ; it is Christ that has made
resurrection. To those who have seen His
beauty, even Olivet can add no certainty; the
light of immortality is as bright on His Cross

as on His Crown. "I *am* the resurrection" are His own words about Himself—not "I teach," not "I cause," not "I predict," but "I am." He thought it almost superfluous to say "In My Father's house are many mansions"; His life should have been itself our light. "If it were not so, I should have told you."

My soul, art thou in doubt about thy future? Art thou searching for a testimony of Christ on the nature of angels? Thou art looking too far. Not His testimony, but His life, shall be thy light. What shall be thy proof of the spring? Not the primrose, not the swallows, not even the sunshine, but the breath within thee of the opening year. No man by searching can find the ivory gate that leads to immortality. There is no method but the method of Jesus—life. He came to the Crown when He was following the Cross; He found the gate of heaven when he was seeking the door of earth. So shall it be with thee, oh, my soul. Is the ivory gate dim to thee? Do not strive to clear thy sight. Forget the gate in the going. Turn thine eyes to the day and to the dust. Turn thine ears to the cry in the desert. Turn thine hands to the labour of the toiling. Turn thy heart to the wants of the weary. And, lo! in the unexpected scene the ivory gate shall shine. The door to God shall open through the dust; the road to Olivet shall glitter in the gloom; and, where the rivers of humanity meet, thou shalt find the way to Paradise. To live the life of Jesus is thy only light.

LVI.

God's Sight of Our Beginnings.

Psalm cxxxix. 2 v.

"Thou understandest my thought afar off."

Love is longsighted; Divine love is the longest sighted. It sees me when I am standing on the very boundary-line between the good and the bad. What is that boundary-line? It is the wish to be. There is a time when I have no virtue but a longing, no gift but an admiration, no soaring but a sigh. I have only drawn the curtains and looked out upon the world of life, and confessed that it is better to be out than in. No common eye would see in me any difference from other men. Who can tell where the last plant ends and the first sentient life begins? Often have I thought of these words, " two shall be grinding at the mill; one shall be taken and the other left." The two are wondrously alike; the locality is the same, the occupation is the same, the outer deed is the same. What makes the difference? To each the mill of the universe utters one sound; both hear the voice of the grinding. But to each it is a separate voice. To the one it is only the mill; to the other it is the music of the mill. One hears but the monotonous hum of daily toil; to the other the mill is saying " bright fields beyond."

And that, oh, my Father, is what Thou hearest, what Thou seest in me. It is a signal at the very end of the line; but Thou readest it afar off. Saul is persecuting the Church, and men are flying from him; but Thou seest in him the signal of need; Thou knowest that he cries for the Christ whom he disclaims. All men can greet me when my light from heaven comes; but to Thee my beginning is the darkness on the face of the deep. In the very warrings of my spirit Thou canst read my attraction to Thy Christ. Thou canst see my conscious blindness long before I reach

Damascus. Thou knowest that my journey to Damascus has been itself a groping, my loudness the loudness of despair, my courage the fear to pause and think. Men hear the grinding, but Thou hearest the music. I would rather have *Thee* than my brother to write my epitaph. My brother waits for Damascus; Thou findest me at Jerusalem. If I die on the road to Damascus, I have no chance from my brother; but even then, Thou shalt see the Paul beneath the persecutor. Unto whom can I go but unto Thee; Thou understandest my thought afar off.

LVII.

Childhood at the Last.

Luke xv. 24 v.

"And they began to be merry."

BEGAN! Was the life of joy only beginning now? The prodigal had expected to find merriment in his youth; he had left his father's house with a view to find it. And had it only come at the end of the day, when youth was gone and the shadows were lengthening? Yes, that is the order of the life of God. We speak of the Wheel of Life; that of the soul is not a wheel, but a triangle. It is heavy at the base and light at the summit. It grows lighter as we climb. The heavy heart is at the beginning —on the ground-floor. As we ascend, the air grows rarer, and, at the top, the soul is buoyant. I used to wonder what was the meaning of these words, " Except ye become as little children, ye shall not enter into the kingdom." It seemed a strange thing that the beginning should be the most glorious time. But now the mystery is clear. If the child is king, it is because the child is latest. The years of time go from youth to manhood; but the years of eternity go from manhood to youth. They are born in conscious struggle, and they culminate in unconscious song. They bud in faith, and they blossom in feeling. Their dawn is the repression of doubt, but their meridian is irrepressible morning. They begin with the knowledge of good and evil; they reach their maturity in the joy of the Lord.

Son of Man, it is after Thy *judgment* the words are spoken, " Enter ye into the joy of your Lord." Thy judgment must come first. I must begin by opening the books and reading the register. It is hard reading; it is reading for a man, not for a child. But I know that the child is coming afterwards, and the book for the child. I know that the days of unconscious play shall be, not my first, but my latest days. I know that Thy morning comes after Thy evening; make haste with Thy morning, oh Lord. I am travelling, not to age, but to youth —not from joy to peace, but from peace to joy. I have begun in the mists of manhood; I have trusted where I cannot trace. One day I shall be a child, and *see;* and then the trees of the forest shall clap their hands. Come, with the light heart of youth. Come, with the wings of the morning. Come, with the river of Thy pleasures. Make me free; make me buoyant; make me gushing; make me a child of Nature; make me a breath of spring. Give me the rose in late autumn, and the song of the swallow in November. I have entered by the strait gate; I have journeyed by the narrow way; when I reach the Father's house I shall begin to be merry.

LVIII.

God in the World.

John xiv. 22 v.

"How is it that Thou wilt manifest Thyself unto us, and not unto the world?"

JUDE was really asking a very common question —how can two men look at the same object and see differently? Yet, they can, and they do. You and I go up together into the temple of Nature—you, with a measuring-rod; I, with a prayer-book. *You* count how long it will take to walk round it; *I* bow before a mystic presence. *You* estimate the weight of the corn —you buy and sell in the temple; *I* am thrilled with a sense of beauty, humbled by an impression of mystery. Yet, we have gazed on the same form. To both it has one size, one colour, one shape. Why do *you* call it the world, and I, the other world? It is because we have brought different worlds into the temple. We draw out of the vision exactly what we put in. *You* have put *in* the seats of the money-changers, and you get out the seats of the money-changers again, accompanied by a scourge of small cords. *I* have put in my belief in the omnipresence of beauty, and I get out its presence from this spot of ground. Nature has manifested herself to me as she has not done to the world.

Who shall see the beauty of Thy face, oh Lord? It is a beauty of the spirit, and can only be read by the spirit. It is not space that veils Thy brightness from any man; it is the thoughts of the heart. That which we call the world is within us; it is not in the air, but in the soul. The world of revelation is not beyond the grave; it is beyond the mire. Not by wings of angels, but by purity of heart, shall we find Thee. We speak of Thee as behind the veil; Thou art only behind the veil of selfishness. Rend the veil of selfishness, and we shall see Thee. We ask not change of place, but change of soul. We are *now* in the midst of Thine eternity; reveal Thyself, oh God. We are gazing on Thy palace, and we think it a stone wall; reveal Thyself, oh God. Reveal the Eternity in Time, the Spirit in Matter, the Gospel in Science, the Church in the World. Reveal the glory of common things,

J

the strength of weak things, the hope of erring things, the mystery of lowly things. Reveal that, as we journey through the way we call the world, we are, all the time, like Thy servant Abraham, wandering unconsciously in the Promised Land.

LIX.

The Sin-bearer.

Isaiah liii. 6 v.

"The Lord hath laid on Him the iniquity of us all."

WHAT a burdened conscience! It must have been the most burdened conscience in the world. Yet, this man was personally sinless. How can we account for the anomaly? How can we reconcile the burden with the blamelessness? Easily; nothing can explain the burden *but* the blamelessness. Do you know what sinlessness is? It is perfect unselfishness. And do you know what perfect unselfishness is? It is the breaking of the partition between my life and other lives. You have a large room, beautifully furnished, and a little ante-room, separated by a wall, and badly furnished. You

[margin handwritten notes: Jesus personally Sinless personally unselfish; reconcile Burden with blamelessness]

break down the wall and make them one room; and you have lost the prestige of your furniture. The large room has taken in the little one with all its imperfections; it has borne its sins. If it were to become conscious, it would be aware of blemishes within it not its own. So was it with the Divine Man. He broke the middle wall of partition between His room and your room. He destroyed the barrier between the large and the small apartment; He made of twain one. He allowed your mean furniture to blend with His costly adornments. He felt your life to be a part of His life. He was mesmerised by love. He looked at His brother's temptations, and said, " They did it unto Me." He bore in His own body the pain of other bodies. It was not the sense of pity; it was the sense of identity—the identity of love. It was His unselfishness that gave Him a universal conscience—" the *Lord* hath laid on Him the iniquity of us all."

Son of Man, let this mind be in me which was also in Thee. It is the sameness of mind that is the test of communion. Thou art never so near to me as when I *think* like Thee. Break the partition between my room and my brother's room. Give me the sense of one apartment—of membership in the same body. Destroy mere pity; it is the barrier-wall from which I look down. Give me the identity of love. Lend me Thy sense of a common life. Create within me the pain of my brother—not the pain *for* him, but the pain that should be *in* him. Inspire me with the remorse which *he* should feel. Impel me to the sacrifice which he should bear. Force me to discharge the debts which he should pay. I shall be nearest life when I have most of Thy death. Thy hand shall be laid very tenderly upon me when Thou hast laid on me my brother's sin.

LX.

God's Architectural Plan.

Matthew xxi. 42 v.

" Did ye never read . . . . the stone which the builders rejected, the same is become the head of the corner ? "

THE book of each man's life is made out of rejected articles. I take up to-day what I laid down yesterday. The sighs of the past have become the songs of the present; the winter from which I fled has met me as my spring. And the large world is like the small. It has mistaken the plan of its own architecture. It found at the beginning a stone which seemed a blemish; it was the stone of sacrifice. How came it there? Men said: "It must have been an accident!—let the building go on without it, let the workmen pass it by." But the tower would not reach to heaven, labour as they might; and the toilers piled in vain. Then they said "Let us try the old stone—the rejected stone." And they picked up from the ground the thing they had cast away, and lo! it fitted all the vast space

between earth and heaven. The accident became the design; the blemish was made the bloom; the interruption proved the finishing-touch of the tower that climbed to God.

Son of Man, Thou symbol and soul of sacrifice, Thou art the architectural plan of this world. Without Thee, not only can we do nothing; we cannot make out what has been done. We have looked at the wrong plan, and the world will not yield it. We have figured skies without clouds, fields without tares, laughter without tears. And the real skies are not cloudless, the real fields are not tareless, the real laughter is not tearless. Hast Thou broken the rainbow of Thy promise? Nay, Thou hast broken *my* bow, not Thine. Thy bow abides in strength, for it is the bow in the cloud. There are no drops so vindicated as tear-drops. I have painted my sea without the waves; but Thou hast made the waves for Thy feet. I have painted my world without the mountains; but Thy steps are beautiful upon the mountains. I have painted my day without a breeze; but Thou ridest upon the wings of the wind. I have painted my morning without a night; but with Thee the evening and the morning are one day. The streets of Thy New Jerusalem are paved with gold, but it is with gold tried in the fire. The stone that sparkled on Olivet was hewn on Calvary.

LXI.

Doubt.

John xx. 13 v.

"They have taken away my Lord, and I know not where they have laid Him."

To whom were these words spoken? To the angels. What a strange audience! One would have said they were more fit for the ears of a society of sceptics. Do not they breathe a spirit of the deepest doubt—a despair of the very *body* of Christ? Why is the doubt, why is the despair, addressed to the angels? Because all honest doubt is prayer, and is borne on high by heavenly messengers. To whom do I cry when I am in doubt? Not to man, surely. I may proclaim my disbelief to a large concourse of men; but, if I am honest, I am speaking only *at* them, not *to* them; my real auditor is God. My cry is the cry to touch the print of the nails. It sounds, below, like a denial; but, above, it is interpreted as a supplication. Men on earth say, "he blasphemeth"; but the angels in heaven exclaim, "Behold, he prayeth."

My soul, art thou troubled with the problems of the mind? Art thou beating against the bars that shut thee out from flight —the flight of prayer? Nay, but the beating is a part of thy flight, a part of thy prayer. Thinkest thou the doubt is thy search for God; it is thy God's search for thee. Only through God canst thou learn the barrier to God. No man would feel imprisoned if he had not an experience of liberty. Why do the wings beat against the cage? If there were nothing seen outside of it, there would be no beating; the cage would be the universe. But when the beyond appears, thou art frantic to be free. It is the sun that makes thy shadow; it is the music that makes thy silence; it is the power of flight that makes thy fetters known. Thy sense of bondage is the vision of the beyond; it is God that makes thy want

of God. Thy cry is a prayer. It is not yet
the prayer of faith, but it is the prayer *for*
faith. It brings nothing in its hand but the
sense of its emptiness; yet God shall take the
hand and fill it with His own. He can read
the Christ beneath the cry. The Christ is
still thy Lord, though, it may be, thou knowest
not where they have laid Him.

LXII.

Christ's Love of Life.

John x. 17 v.

"Therefore doth My Father love Me, because I lay
down My life, that I might take it again."

"THAT I might take it again." The beauty of
Christ's sacrifice is not its despair. Despair is a
spectacle which the Father never loves to see.
How could He? Does an artist love to see his
work despised? Life is God's work, and He
deems it beautiful. How could He love a man
because he wished to lay it down? The desire
for death is not a "sacrifice of praise"; it is a
criticism on the work of the Father. But if

death is desired for the sake of life, it makes all
the difference. If death is sought, not because
life is sad, but because life is dear, then the
search for death is a tribute to the Father. So
was it with the Son of Man. None felt like
Him the glory of living. Life was so beautiful
that He was willing to die for it. Not in grief,
but in prospective joy, did He yield Himself to
the Cross. If He had despaired more, He would
have sacrificed less. It was the worth, and not
the worthlessness, of living that made Him die.
His dying was an act of praise to the Giver of
life; therefore, the Giver of life loved it. He
laid existence down that He might take it again.

My soul, dost thou know what this meaneth:
" Enter ye into the joy of your Lord " ? Thinkest
thou that the joy of thy Lord is something
which comes after the sacrifice ? No ; it is that
which prompts the sacrifice. Are not thy deepest
sacrifices prompted by a joy ? Whence thy
laborious nights of study ? They are from joy
—the joy of possibly seeing the opened heavens.
Whence thy self-denying poverty ? It is from
joy—the joy of saving to make another rich.
Whence thy sojourn in lane and alley, in the
homes of misery and the haunts of sin ? It is

from joy—the joy of perhaps beholding the spirits in prison set free. Do not wait for thy Lord's joy until the battle is over and the victory won. It is for the battle that thou needest it. Nothing can conquer death but the love of something in life. It is by the rose thou shalt bear thy thorn. It is by the sun thou shalt meet thy cloud. It is by the calm thou shalt face thy storm. It is by the bread of to-morrow thou shalt brave the hunger of to-day. It is thy star that guides thee to thy cross; the flame that lights thy fire is the torch of hope. If thou wouldst sustain the winter's cold, thou must bathe first in the summer warmth. Let not thy life go down till thou canst take it again.

LXIII.

Enrichment by Christ's Poverty.

2 Corinthians viii. 9 v.

" He became poor, that ye through His poverty might be rich."

ALL love is enriched by the poverty of its object. My love to the Divine is no exception. If my God comes to me in trappings of gold, it is a light thing that I should follow him. If to be good is to be on the sunny side, if virtue brings to me a large dowry, a poor love may suffice to make me her own. But if she come penniless, landless, if her gold has become dim, if her dowry has been proved a delusion, if she can only ask me to share her struggle and her toil, the love that can respond with consent must be rich indeed.

Oh, Thou Divine Spirit, I bless Thee that by Thy poverty Thou hast enriched my love. Often in the days of old hast Thou come to me with the purple, and the fine linen, and the sumptuous faring; and I was glad to be with Thee, not because Thou wert beautiful, but because Thou wert profitable. I arose and followed Thee because I left nothing. But now Thou appearest in mean attire. The purple and fine linen are exchanged for sackcloth and ashes. The crown has been cast into the sea, the glory has been buried in the dust, and, in its room, Thou carriest a cross of great pain. My old nature shrinks back from Thee; Thou art no more the spirit of its dream. But, as it sleeps, my heart waketh. My new life rises on the ruins of the old. My love becomes rich as Thou becomest poor; I find my star in Thy night. I come to Thee in the gate of Golgotha; I meet Thee in the place of tears; I join Thee in the valley of humiliation; I descend with Thee to the spirits in prison. Where Thou goest I shall go. Death itself shall not separate between Thee and me. Death with Thee were worth eternity without Thee; pain with Thee were worth joy without Thee; hell with Thee were worth heaven without Thee. Thou art the only pearl in my sea; Thou art the only gem in my sky; Thou art the only song in my soul. Pilate may divest Thee of Thy robes, but he cannot rob Thee of Thy beauty. My love can see Thy kinghood in Thy cross; Thy poverty has made me rich.

LXIV.

The Spiritual in the Earthly.

John xx. 15 v.

"Supposing Him to be the gardener."

Nature answers in refrain to thee — to thy sorrows and to thy joys

WE often mistake Christ for the gardener— attribute to mere physical beauty what comes from faith alone. We speak of the glories of Nature ; most of its glories belong to man. We find a sense of infinitude in the breath of the new-mown hay ; yet, truly, it is not in that, but in *thee*. It has been said : " Thou weavest for God the garment by which thou seest Him " ; more justly might the words be spoken of Nature. Her song is the echo of thy song. She answers in refrain to thee—to thy sorrows and to thy joys. Often have men exhorted thee to follow the teachings of Nature, and to look on the things beyond as an idle dream. Nay, but thy vision of Nature depends on thy vision of grace. In vain shalt thou seek in the flower the grace which is not in thy soul. It is from the things beyond the earth that earthly beauty flows. The voice which thou hearest in the garden is the voice of the Lord. That which uplifts thee in the flower is just what the gardener has not planted. It is the life below the stem, the mystery beneath the root. It is the sense of a presence which has escaped the eye, of a power which has eluded the botanist. It is the feeling that the gardener has planted something which he has not seen—a seed from the life eternal, a blossom from the breast of God.

Oh, Thou, whose Easter morning shines in many disguises, help me to recognise Thee everywhere. Let me not ascribe to the gardener the work that is done by Thee. I often speak of the noble lives led by men who do not know Thee; teach me that Thou knowest *them*. Tell me that Thy presence is wider than our creed, Thy temple bigger than our sanctuary, Thy love larger than our law. Convince me that Thou enfoldest that which does not enfold *Thee*. Let me learn that Thou art the one "excellent name in all the earth." Men call their excellent things by other names; they take Thee to be the gardener. Hasten the time when they shall take the gardener to be Thee; they shall be nearer to the ·truth of things. Hasten the time when " in the *flesh* they shall see God "—see Him in

The mystery beneath the root

the forms of earth, see Him in the duties of the hour, see Him in the paths of life, see Him in the progress of the day. Make Thyself known to them in the breaking of the earthly bread; in the planting of the earthly flower let them gaze on *Thee.*

LXV.

The Strength beyond Nature.

Psalm viii. 1, 2 v.

"O Lord .... who hast set Thy glory above the heavens. Out of the mouth of babes and sucklings hast Thou ordained strength .... that Thou mightest still the .... avenger."

THE Psalmist says that when he considers only the heavens, he cries: "What is man, that Thou art mindful of him?" So do all of us; it is a very bad thing to keep the eye exclusively on masses of matter. Whenever you are oppressed, he says, by the glory of the heavens, you ought to remember that there is a "glory *above* the heavens." Whenever you feel dwarfed by the strength of nature, remember that there is a strength which, though ascribed to the babe, is higher than nature. What is that strength? It is the thing called meekness—the thing that stills the avenger in the breast. We uncover our heads in wonder before the stilling of a natural storm. But the stilling of a soul-storm is more wonderful far. In the most obscure heart there is a tempest unrecorded—a tempest before which nature itself would quail. Yet the obscure heart conquers it, calms it, and is called a weakling for its victory. We revere the strength of the summer day because it holds the storm on its bosom. But we forget the strength of many a gentle spirit whose smile conceals the rain, whose flower has hid the thorn, whose calm restrains the torrent, whose meekness stills the avenger within.

Son of Man, set Thy glory to me above the heavens. Teach me the majesty of Thy meekness. I do not ask a still nature; what I want is a stilling nature. I would not have a soul where there is nothing to restrain. That is the peace the world gives—the peace of spent passion, the peace of exhausted energy. But not as the world givest Thou. Thine is not a sea of glass; it is glass mingled with fire. I would not lose the fire, oh, Christ of Calvary; I would be calmed

K

through the fire—through the very burning of my love. Beautifully was it written that the meekest man started from the burning bush. I need great strength to make me gentle. If I would have Thy dove of peace, I must have Thy vision of Jordan. Any clod of the valley can *be* still; but only the sight of the mountain can *make* still. The sea of my life is not calmed by diminishing the waters, but by the print of Thy footsteps treading thereon. I shall reach Thy patience when I have possessed my soul; I shall still my heart when Thou hast made me strong.

LXVI.

The Finality of Christ.

Romans vi. 9 v.

"Christ being raised from the dead, dieth no more."

A BOLD assertion; the man who made it must have been a great man. In a world of change, in an age of special changes, he declared that the human race had reached finality. This faith in the Crucified, he says, will be the last religion. Men will never outgrow it, never get beyond it.

Times shall change, manners shall change, customs shall change, the order of life shall change; but this faith shall abide. The heavens shall pass away with a loud noise. A new science of the stars shall dawn. The earth shall move round the sun instead of the sun moving round the earth. But there shall be no new Christ in the firmament; His eye shall not grow dim, His strength shall not be abated. A thousand systems shall fall at His side, but their crash shall not touch *Him.* He shall be the survivor in the struggle for existence. He shall have the dew of His youth when the world is old. He shall have the last judgment. There shall be no verdict after His, no appeal to the Cæsar of a future age. His feet shall touch the final ridge of the mountains, and the beauty of His tidings shall be a joy for ever.

Oh, Thou, who art the latest flower of the garden, I am glad that I can rest in Thee. My heart is weary of its wandering. Scarce has it found an hour's repose. Oft has it sat down by the wayside dreaming that its work was done; and a gleam from beyond has said, "Arise and depart, for this is not thy rest." Therefore I am glad that at last I see no beyond. Hope is beautiful, but satisfaction is better; and I shall be satisfied with Thy likeness. No likeness shall ever eclipse it. I do not need to look forward any more, not even to heaven. Heaven is not beyond me when Thou art beside me. Faith and hope are lost when love to Thee is found. There is no morrow to Thy love, any more than there is evening. Thou Thyself mayst grow brighter; but no brighter than Thee shall come. When I have reached the vision of Thee, I shall for the first time live in the present—be a child of the hour. The butterfly's wing shall be mine when I soar in *Thy* air. Without Thee, my sigh has been for to-morrow ; *with* Thee, my cry shall be, " *Now* is the accepted time, now is the day of salvation."

LXVII.

The Humility of Greatness.

John x. 4 v.

" When he putteth forth his own sheep, he goeth before them."

THERE is a time in the Christian life when God puts us forth—brings us out into the great world. But our Lord says that this period of advancement is the time when we feel most in the rear—" when He putteth forth His own sheep, He goeth before them." We never see Christ so far in advance of us as in the time of our own progress ; the man who comes nearest to Him says that he follows afar off. No one feels himself so little a leader as the great man. Small men have no guiding star ; they walk by their own light. But the sage will not journey till he has seen his star. He is of all men the humblest, the most reverent, the most fearful. He uncovers his head beneath skies purer than his own ; he bends before the mystery which he sees, but cannot solve ; he prays beside the sea whose margin his feet have touched.

Son of Man, ever let me feel that Thou art before me. Thou art always before me, but I have not always felt it. I was very proud in my small days. Ere yet I had been enlarged by Thee, I had no shrinking in my nature. I pitied the past, and proposed to set it right; I pitied the present, and purposed to excel it. But when I was put forth, brought out, given a post in advance, then it was that I felt humble. The flower of my life turned to the sun when it began to blossom; in its ripeness it looked to Thee. The proof of its summer was its sense of impotence, of inability to stand alone. Never let me lose this sense of impotence, this evidence of the kindled flower. Never let me lose that want of Thee which is the pledge that I am nearing Thee. I am only *in*spired when I have *a*spired—sighed for something above me. When I first saw Thee, I thought it was a light thing to reach Thee; I said, "Bid me that I come to Thee on the waters." But now the stream has become a river, and the river has widened into a sea, and Thou art far before. Teach me it is a message of hope, not despair. Tell me I am never so close to Thee as when love throws its seeming gulf between. Reveal to me that when the hills look far away it is a sign that the rain is over. It is the putting forth of my soul that sends Thee on before.

LXVIII.

Christian Union.

Isaiah lii. 8 v.

"They shall see eye to eye, when the Lord shall bring again Zion."

AND so, vision is the last thing! I had always thought that men must see eye to eye before they were ransomed. Here, the ransom comes first, and the agreement afterwards. And truly it must be so. It is the captivity that hinders union. We do not see eye to eye, because we are all in separate cells. Each man's cell is to him the universe. We see only one side of the Christ—that which breaks our special chain. *I* am oppressed by the fear of penalty; *you* are laden with the dread of being overlooked. *I* am weighted by the thought of the future; *you* are saddened by the clouds of the present. I am in search of a power; you are sighing for a tenderness. I am in terror for the cup of Dives; you are seeking for the cup of Gethsemane. I disparage your Christ and your cry; I say it is not the gospel. It is not the gospel for *my* captivity, and I forget your captivity. I cannot see the whole Christ in my narrow cell; I see only the little bit that suits me. If I could get out, I would behold his fulness; if God would break my door, I would see your door. Fear casteth out perfect love, and, therefore, perfect light. The key which opens my brother's prison does not open mine; I want mine to be opened, and I quarrel with the key. I cannot preach your gospel till I have lost my own chain. We shall see eye to eye when the Lord's freedom has returned to Zion.

My Father, let me not wait for the union of the eye. I bless Thee that there is an earlier union. I bless Thee that the marriage of the heart precedes the marriage of the mind. I bless Thee that men can meet in love ere they are able to meet in faith. I cannot see Thee eye to eye with my brother; but the very difference may unite us. Is it not written that there is a " fellowship in the *mystery* "? I thank Thee for that fellowship. My brother and I can be united by the thing we do not see. Help him and me to feel that each of us looks only on a fragment. Unite us by the limits of our eye. Join us by the clouds over our vision. Bring us together at our sunset—where each of our lights goes down. Put our hands in one in the spot where our experience is severed. Let us walk together through the night till the time comes when we shall walk by day. Let us meet at the barriers of the life till we can bask in the revelations of the soul. When the gates are opened, we shall see eye to eye.

LXIX.

The Blemishes Revealed by Light.

Genesis xxxii. 31 v.

"As he passed over Penuel the sun rose upon him, and he halted upon his thigh."

WHAT a strange combination!—darkness and light. As he passed over the place of his former struggle he had a double experience— "the sun rose upon him," and, "he halted upon his thigh." There was at one and the same

moment a blaze and a blemish—glory around
his head, and weakness in his walk. Was there
a contradiction in the sight? No; it is the
law of the Divine life. Our halt is never felt
till the sun rises, not clearly seen till the sun
rises. There are no blemishes so marked as the
blemishes of a purified soul. When the whole
pool is stagnant, the special impurity is not
seen; but when the cleansing is far advanced,
one speck becomes marvellous. I never look so
humble to my fellow-men as when the sun of
Penuel is over me. Its very brightness shows
the faults in my form. Men talk more of my
one evil deed than of the ninety-and-nine evil
deeds of those that never saw Penuel, that
never knew the rising of the sun. They say:
" He must be a hypocrite. How can the
lambent flame enwrap the lame figure? Can
the head of the image be of gold when the feet
are of contemptible clay? "

Yes, it can; and for this I thank Thee, oh,
my Father. I thank Thee that the halting in
my step does not imply that the sun is not
risen. Often have I been distressed by the
survivals of my dead self; I have met on the
mountain what I fancied I had left in the

valley. Yet, I am not therefore disloyal to Thee, untrue to Thee. Two lives are in me— the old and the new. In the city of Thy New Jerusalem there are vacant spaces that tell of an olden time. They tell of a time when there was no city, when it was all open-country and silent fields. Gradually, Thy city is breaking my solitude. Step by step the silent fields are being invaded, and the voices of the crowd are filling the waste places of my heart. Thou hast not yet come up with me, oh, my Father; Thy New Jerusalem is only building, and the wastes wait for Thee. To-morrow, they shall be vocal. To-morrow, a multitude shall clap their hands where the trees of the forest once stood. To-morrow, the streets shall be paved, and the feet shall tread unspotted over the miry clay. To-day, the halting and the sunshine are side by side. When Thy city shall reach its bounds, I shall traverse, as well as see, the path of gold.

LXX.

A Prayer for Enemies.

Psalm ix. 20 v.

"Put them in fear, O Lord, that the nations may know themselves to be but men."

"PUT them in fear"—is that a prayer for an inspired book? Is it humane to ask that my enemies may be put in fear? Yes, if it is to make them *human*. The Psalmist asks God to teach his enemies "that they are but men"—to teach them pity for others by showing them the weak point in themselves. He feels that they want sympathy because they want experience. No man can bring help to the clouded heart unless he has made the clouds his chariot. It is only through sorrow that I can comfort sorrow. The shut door of my experience is the door that shuts me in. The tears which I shed for my brother must be tears of memory. Their fountain must lie in the yesterday of my heart. If I have no yesterday, I have no tears. I cannot put myself in my brother's place unless I have *been* in his place. My pity is an echo of my past, and where there is no past there is no pity. If the halls of memory are silent, the voice of sympathy is dead. The night that appeals to my compassion must be painted on the canvas of a vanished day.

Therefore, oh, my Father, I am not afraid to pray for the unsympathetic " put them in fear." I am not afraid to say, "make them more humane, by teaching them to be more human." I am not afraid to wish them the good gift of Thy chariot-clouds. I know that Thy clouds would enlarge them—give them more driving room. I know they would carry them further down the road of humanity, further up the steep of Calvary. I know they would bear them through gates that have long been closed—gates of the heart, that keepeth its own bitterness, and forbiddeth a stranger to intermeddle therewith. Shall I not wish such enlargement, even to my foe? Is not this the enlargement, my Father, that Thou wishest for *Thy* foe—this heart of mine, alien to love? It is for this Thou sendest into my days so many pillars of cloud; Thou wouldest make me a pillar to the clouded. It is for this Thou puttest fear within me—that I may know myself to be only a man. It is for this Thou spreadest the canvas of sorrow—that my brother's night may be pictured in my soul. It is for this Thou lendest the labour and the ladenness—that I may learn the secret of giving rest. I bless Thee for Thy gift of sympathetic fear.

LXXI

The Flower Below the Thorn.

Matthew xiii. 7 v.

"Some fell among thorns; and the thorns sprung up, and choked them."

THE seed fell among thorns; it fell into a heart which had not been emptied of its troubles. If the seed had been there first, it would have made all the difference. There is a place for the thorn. Every rose has its thorn; but the rose is in the bud, and the thorn is on the surface. Christ had His thorn—His crown of thorns; but peace was at the root, and they could not mar His beauty. It is not a question of whether I shall or shall not have trouble. I must have trouble; I cannot escape it; I may not safely pray to escape it. My life without the cross would be a poor life, a maimed life, a worthless life. But my cross is not to be my first visitor. It is to have something below it, underlying it, bearing it. I am to wear my thorn where Christ wore it—on a heart of love. No one can forbid the thorn to *occupy*, if only the flower shall *preoccupy ;* trouble may visit my house, if the Master has first come in. But do not let the trouble lie below. Do not let it be next the heart, closest to the breast. Do not let there be nothing beneath it, nothing to support it. Do not let it rest on the threshold and bar the entrance to the soul. Everything depends on the entrance ; be sure you plant your flower ere you admit your thorn.

Come, then, into my heart, Thou Rose of Sharon ; be the first visitor of all my year. Let my thorn fall upon Thy life—not Thy life upon my thorn. If Thou fallest on my thorn, Thy fragrance shall be broken ; I shall see no beauty that I can desire in Thee. But if Thou shalt lie next to my heart, I can let my thorn fall on *Thee.* It will not break Thy fragrance ; it may even catch Thy fragrance ; it may become a part of Thee. Come into my heart ; come and anticipate the thorn. Come with the star of the morning, ere the heat and the burden arise. Come with the song of the lark, ere the wheels of traffic are heard. Come with the glow of the east, where the day is yet far from its setting. Come with the promise of youth, where the bow is apart from the flood. And the star shall lift the burden, and the song shall help the traffic, and the glow shall gild the setting, and the bow shall assuage the flood. There is room for my thorn above Thy seed; let not Thy seed fall upon my thorn.

LXXII.

The Cosmetic for the Soul.

Mark ix. 49 v.

" Every one shall be salted with fire."

To be salted is to be preserved—kept young. How to keep young, is a great problem. Our Lord says that the soul needs an opposite cosmetic from the body. The cosmetic for the body is to take care of one's self, to keep out of danger, to avoid the path of trouble. But

the cosmetic for the soul is to take no care
of one's self, to seek the danger of another,
to court the path of trouble. Christ gives
youth as He gives peace—in a manner different
from that of the world. He makes us little
children by laying His hands upon us, by
giving us a new weight—the weight of love.
It is not by the heart's lightness but by the
heart's pressure that He makes us young. My
body groans beneath its burden; but my
spirit groans when it has no burden. There
is no weariness to my spirit like the absence
of care. The oldest heart is the fetterless
heart. If it be not in bonds, it is in de-
crepitude. Its youth only comes when its
chain comes. Like the men of ancient Babylon,
it only ceases to be hurt when it passes through
the furnace. It is the true Phœnix-Bird; it
rises out of its own ashes. It is born again
from the altar of sacrifice. It is renewed
by the flame that consumes it. It is salted
with fire.

Preserve me, oh Lord; keep me young.
Thou hast an elixir that makes fair for ever;
its name is love. It makes fair by strange
methods; when I have tasted it, I shall be on

L

fire. Martyrs have passed through the flames to life eternal—life that never grows old. Men tell me the need has passed away with the days of persecution; teach me it is not so. Teach me that the only persecutor of my youth is the spirit of selfishness. Teach me that the Herod who would kill the young child within me is the same yesterday, and to-day, and for ever. Teach me that the road to life eternal is still through the fire. Teach me that if I would be kept young, it must be through the cares of love. Redeem me from old age by the blood of Thy Cross. Restore my morning by the setting of my own sun. Bring back my spring-time by the burial of my selfish seed. Renew my childhood by an entrance into other lives. My heart can only be preserved by sacrifice; it shall resume its youth in Thy everlasting fire.

LXXIII.

Christic in Everything.

Revelation iii. 12 v.

" He shall go no more out."

Is there then to be no more liberty? Is the
penalty of my conquest to be my own captivity?
Am I to be imprisoned within the golden gate
that my own victory has opened? Not so;
you can go where you like; the world shall
be yours. Why, then, is it said, " He shall
go no more out"? Simply because there shall
be no more anything outside; the whole
universe shall be enclosed in Christ. You
shall never get beyond your walls; but your
walls shall enfold creation. You shall never
escape from God's presence; but you shall
find God's presence everywhere. The tree of
knowledge shall be no longer forbidden; the
tree of life shall be no longer barred. You
shall walk to the limits of earth, and find it
an Eden. The Cross of Christ shall be in
every street; the altar of sacrifice shall be

L 2

in every pleasure. There shall be nothing secular to you, nothing worldly, nothing frivolous. You will not need to fly from the old scenes into the sanctuary; the old scenes shall themselves be the sanctuary. You will not need to shut your door on the world when you go up to pray; the world shall itself be your house of prayer. You shall worship when you work; you shall pray when you practise; you shall love when you labour. Your ledger shall be a book of devotion; you shall be at Church on 'Change. Your social call shall be a ministrant visit—a healing of present wounds. The songs you sing shall all be sacred songs— not from their subject, but from their motive; you will sing to make glad. The days you spend shall all be Sabbath days; you shall not cease from work, but you shall cease from worry. The pastimes you enjoy shall all be sacrificial pastimes—the sympathy with another's joy. You will be found in many a scene beneath you, many a surmounted pleasure. You will learn that joy as well as sadness was made for the Cross of Jesus. You shall throw yourself into the interest of others— interest which perhaps has long since faded from your ascending day. You shall bring trifling things within the gates of gold by the very act of bending to them. The feast of Cana is a trifle to *you;* but it is something to somebody. If you can throw yourself into that lower experience, you have put Christ in Cana. If you can remember that the trifle of to-day was the treasure of yesterday, and see your brother's world in the light of long ago, you may dwell in the things of time, and not go out from Jesus.

LXXIV.

The Gain of Loss.

Philemon i. 15 v.

"Perhaps he therefore departed for a season, that thou shouldest receive him forever."

THERE are possessions which only become our own when for a time we have lost them. There are joys which never abide with us till they have passed through the cloud. We, like Philemon, are enriched by our bereavements. We often hold a faith just because we have

[left margin handwritten note:] Possessions become Ours only one for a time we have lost them

[right margin handwritten note:] Joys abide with us after we have passed through the clouds

been born to it; and its value is unknown. But a cloud comes and receives it out of our sight; and suddenly it becomes precious. We awake to the knowledge that there has been a diamond in our hand. We find that we have been rich without knowing it. We would give all the world to get back what yesterday we deemed of no price. And in that very desire we are richer, better than we were before. It is better to know the preciousness of faith, even while not having it, than to have it and not know its preciousness. It is better to cry for a Christ whom you believe to be absent than to stand in His presence and count it a worthless thing. And the very cry will bring Him back; for what is thy need of Him but Himself within thee? The cry will bring Him back—no longer to be ignored, but to be cherished; no longer to be an appendage to life, but to be life itself; no longer to be a Sunday guest, but to abide with you forever.

My Father, help me to realise the gain of my losses. I speak of the silver lining in the cloud; teach me that the cloud itself is the silver lining of my life. My life is colourless until Thy cloud comes. It is in the moment of departure that I recognise my angel; the wings are revealed in the act of disappearing. Men say Thou art manifested by what Thou givest; I think Thou art more manifested by what Thou withdrawest. The veil is never so rent from my heart as in the hour when Thou claimest back Thine own. Thy gift becomes most glorious when Thou coverest it with Thy hand; it is expedient for me that my Christ should go away. Thy gifts are too near me to be seen by me. Therefore, Thou hast sent a cloud over the mountain of radiance. Thou hast trained my love by loss; Thou hast educated my faith by shadow; Thou hast taught me morning by night. Thou hast made me to stretch out my hands to clasp that which was unfelt before. Thou hast hid Thyself behind the curtain, that I may learn to cry for Thee. I basked at first in Thee, like an unconscious flower; Thy winter broke the flower, and made me a man. I woke to Thee by the blast of my own wailing—the wailing for an absent joy. I could not take Thy blessing till it had departed for a while.

LXXV.

The Answer to Prayer.

Psalm xx. 6 v.

" Now know I that the Lord saveth His anointed; He will hear him from His holy heaven with the saving strength of His right hand."

THE deepest answer to prayer is not a voice— not a " yes " or a "no "; it is the support of a hand. This is not the common view. I cry to God in the night, and strain through the silence for a message. I never doubt that the answer shall be a voice, never dream that the reply shall be aught but a consent or a denial. I have asked the removal of a trouble; I assume that it will either be granted or refused. Not so thinks the Psalmist. His best hope for prayer is neither the one nor the other. He says that God answers His anointed souls, not by a voice, but by a hand—not directly, but in-directly. There comes from the silent skies no peal of music; there flashes through the outward dark no gleam of glory; but into the heart there steals a strange strength, an unaccountable peace.

Perhaps it was not felt at once. You were in search of another kind of answer, and may not have recognised its coming. It seemed to grow up naturally, to be a bit of yourself, to have nothing superhuman in it. It was not like an answer to prayer at all—it was so woven with your ordinary life. Yet, it was God's own messenger, the response to your cry of yesterday. You spoke to God through one door, and He answered you by another; you opened at the front, and He came in at the back; you asked to be lifted into heaven, and He gave you more power to live on earth; you craved melody for the ear, and He sent you, instead, the saving strength of His right hand.

Son of Man, I accept the answer that was given to *Thee*. Thy cup did not pass, but Thy angel came. Thy angel came by the back door, when Thou wert weeping at the front. He came before Thy tears were ended. The answer to Thy prayer entered Thy heart unseen. It was born in the hour of sorrow; it grew up while Thy tears were falling; but when it was full-grown, there was a great calm. Let me believe that Thy angel is mine. When I pour forth my soul in strong crying and tears, let me believe that the answer is already come. I am looking too far to find it. I seek it in the clearing of the cloud; I expect it in the spilling of the cup; my eye is all on the front, and I forget the postern door. Let me remember *Thee*—Thy Gethsemane, Thy triumph. It is not a new cup I need; it is a new hand. I want something to keep the cup from trembling, yea, from spilling. I want power to hold it calmly, steadily. I want a hand to repress the shaking of my hand. I want none of its drops to fall idly, ineffectually. I want to receive Thy cup in Thy garden — in the power of Thy peace. My prayers shall all be answered when I am answered like Thee.

LXXVI.

The Enforced Reign of Christ.

1 Corinthians xv. 25 v.

"He must reign, till He hath put all enemies under His feet."

"HE *must* reign"; it is not natural to Christ that He should be a king. He feels more humiliation in being a king than in being a servant. To serve is His nature; to reign is His necessity. Love never finds pleasure in reigning. It can do it; it is often compelled to do it; but it does not like to do it. There is a time in which every father *must* reign, in which love has no option but to rule. The child is aiming deadly weapons against itself, throwing destructive missiles in the face of its brother. What can love do but intervene? It cannot allow the reign of love-lessness; it is bound to make for itself a throne. Yet, it longs for other days. It longs to lay its sceptre in the dust. It longs for the time when the child shall forget its empire and remember only its beauty. The sweetest morning to any father is when there is nothing to reign over.

That is always his Easter morning. He wakes
and finds the offering already on his altar. The
flowers have come in spontaneously. The tasks
are done unbidden. The errands are run by
instinct. The wants are met by anticipation
The law has given place to the prophets. The
Ten Commandments remain unspoken; for the
heart of the child has seen the desire of the
parent afar off, and the parent says, "I need
reign no more."

Son of Man, I understand Thy reluctance to
be made a king. I understand how the crown of
David was Thy cross. Thou camest to minister;
it was stern necessity that made Thee reign.
None of Thy crowns is so thorny as the crown of
Thy power. Thy brow is more lacerated by the
symbol of empire than by any human pain.
Thy pain is the need to rule. Thy cross is
to feel Thyself upon the mountain. Thou art
weary of the high level, weary of the height
above Thy brothers. Thou wouldst fain come
down to the plain, down to the valley; nay,
rather, Thou wouldst fain that the valley would
come up to Thee. Thy mountain is Thy
solitude; Thy empire is Thy loneliness. Thou
waitest for all to be one with Thee, to break Thy

pre-eminence, to make Thy kingdom void. Thou waitest for all to feel with Thee, think with Thee, speak with Thee, move with Thee. Thou waitest to cast Thy crown into the sea, and live in hearts responsive to Thine own. Thou wouldst rather knock for admittance at the door than stand for homage on the hill; Thou shalt enter into Thy glory when Thou shalt cease to be a king.

LXXVII.

Exaltation and Revelation.

Acts ii. 33 v.

" Therefore being by the right hand of God exalted . . . He hath shed forth this, which ye now see and hear."

CHRIST's influence came after His exaltation; His Spirit was shed when He was raised on high. Is it not ever so? It is gladness that makes us diffusive. When the burden presses upon us we cannot radiate the good that is in us. We may send out our thought, but it is a weighted thought; it has no wings. Our exalted moments are our revealing moments. We never

shed so much light on ourselves as when transfigured by joy.   Calvary is the time for bearing;
Olivet is the time for revealing.   We open not
our mouth in the world's judgment-hall; when
oppressed and afflicted, we are dumb.   But when
the oppression is lifted, when the affliction is
vindicated, when the spirit is exalted, then the
gates are unbarred and the procession of thought
comes forth.   Grief itself is only revealed when
it touches the sunbeam.   It has no expression
in its utmost depth.   There is needed a gleam
of hope to wake it into tears.   " My voice shalt
thou hear in the morning " is true of all revealings.   It is from the morning of my heart that
my power of utterance comes; I am only made
vocal by the dawn.   " Being exalted, He hath
shed forth this."

How shall I shed forth Thy Spirit, oh, Son of
Man ?   Only when I have reached Thy joy.
Thy Cross is not attractive to men unless Thou
art *lifted up* on it.   The world is not naturally
drawn to scenes of gloom.   The contagious
presence is the joyous presence.   It is not Thy
sorrow that I worship; it is Thy peace in
sorrow—not Thy night, but Thy star.   Forbid
that I should show Thy night without Thy star.

Forbid that I should magnify depression, or extol the path of tears. Forbid that my brother should see my faith as a thing that makes me sad. Thou makest the clouds Thy chariot; but I love not Thy chariot, but Thee. Let me pass behind the veil, that I may radiate Thy light. Let me enter into Thy joy, that Thy Spirit may have wings. Let me tread the green pastures, that Thy footprints may be beautiful. Let me scan the still waters, that Thy rest may be revealed. Give me Thy songs in the night, that the night-watchers may come to hear. Give me Thy bow in the cloud, that the cloud-bearers may come to see. Give me Thy uplifting in my cross, that they who are crushed by *their* cross may learn to hope. I shall have power to shed Thy influence when I am myself exalted.

LXXVIII.

Thanksgiving.

1 Thessalonians v. 18 v.

"In everything give thanks."

SURELY this is a hard saying! Am I to thank God for everything? Am I to thank Him for bereavement, for pain, for poverty, for toil? I may believe that the time will come when I *shall* thank Him; that is an act of faith. But am I to turn faith into fruition? Must I celebrate the victory before the battle? Must I lift up my hands over my dead and say, "Father, I thank Thee that Thou hast taken away my friend"? Is it possible? is it human? is it desirable? Is it the will of Love that love should violate its own law? Is it pleasing to my Father that loss should be pleasant to me? Is my heart to make no distinction between the sunshine and the cloud? Is not one half of my joy just the absence of pain? if I cease to shrink from pain, how shall I keep my joy? Is it good that I should be told to give thanks for everything?

Be still, my soul; thou hast misread the message. It is not to give thanks for everything, but to give thanks *in* everything. It is not to praise God for the night, but to bless Him that the night is not deeper. Bethink thee; thou hast never reached the absolute depth of any darkness, never come to the step which has no step below it. I have read of the Son of Man that He gave thanks over the symbol of His broken body. What does that prove? That He rejoiced in being sad? No, but that He was not perfectly sad. It tells me that even the Man of Sorrows had not reached the uttermost sorrow. Not for the pain, but for the mitigation of the pain, did the Son of Man give thanks—not that His body was broken, but that it was broken for me. In thine hour of sorrow, give thanks like Jesus. Keep thine eye, not on the step above, but on the step below—the step to which thou hast not yet descended. Look not up at the height thou has lost; look down on the depth thou hast not sounded. There might have been no ram caught in thy thicket. There might have been no dream dreamt in thy dungeon. There might have been no bush burning in thy desert. Herod

M

might have come without the sages; Bethlehem might have come without the angels; Judas might have come without the Passover; Calvary might have come without the garden. Thy Father has never allowed the uttermost deep of misery to any human spirit; the cable may creak and strain, but it is anchored within the veil. God never fills the cup of Jesus to the brim; there is always a vacant space reserved for light and air. Is it not written that He has put my tears into His bottle; the quantity of thy griefs is measured; there is a bound which they cannot pass? Thank God for that boundary, oh, my soul.

[handwritten margin note: Cable anchored within the veil]

[handwritten margin note: Boundary of grief is limited by Jesus]

LXXIX.

The Highest Type of Beauty.

Psalm xxiv. 6 v.

"This *is* the generation of them that seek Him, that seek thy face, O Jacob."

THE Psalmist says it was a time of religious revival. Men were seeking God. They were seeking Him in a particular way. They were in search of the illumination that lit up the face of Jacob when he saw God's face. Where was that? It was at Peniel. It was Jacob's third vision of God. He had seen Him at Bethel in His dreadfulness; he had seen Him at Mahanaim in His providence; but at Peniel he saw Him in His communion. He beheld Him face to face, and his own face caught the glow. It was the nearest sight of God that mortal man had ever won. It was nearer even than the view of Adam in the garden. That was in the cool of the day; this was in the burden and the heat. That was before the battle; this was after the fight. That was the gaze of innocence; this was the look of conquering virtue. It is

M 2

something to see God when the heart is young, when life wears the aspect of the garden flower. But to get the vision when the heart is old, to see the divine face after the human struggle, to hear the voice of the Lord, not in the garden, but in the city of earthly care—that is worth a generation's search; that is the communion of Jacob.

My Father, there is a type of beauty which I would like to possess—the face that has seen Thy face. It is independent of feature. It is Jacob after the struggle, and bearing the traces of the struggle; it can shine amid the halting and the lameness of the outward man. It is Thy fairest gift of beauty to a human form and to a human soul, for it is the loveliness of love. I can only reach it by gazing on *Thee;* one touch of self-remembrance would make the picture void. And, should I reach it, it will attract to *Thee* rather than to me. Men will not call it fair; they will term it good. It will be recognised as belonging to *Thy* world, not to mine. Even so, Father; I desire it should speak for *Thee.* I would take it for Thy cause; I would hold it for Thy glory. I would prize it, not for its power to glitter, but for its power to gladden. I would keep it as a magnet to draw the world to Thee. I would like it to be seen best in the times of my struggle and my weakness, for then it would be seen not to belong to me. I would like it to be viewed as something which was above me, and which, therefore, any man might have. I would like it to tell the toiling that Thou canst meet them in their toil. I would like the victims of human struggle to know that Thou hast a beauty for the faded flower, a garment of praise for the spirit of heaviness, and that there is no light so lovely as the light at evening-time. Therefore it is that I seek the face of Jacob.

LXXX.

Love without Dissimulation.

Romans xii. 9 v.

"*Let* love be without dissimulation."

THE words are commonly understood to mean, "Don't pretend you love when you do not"; I would rather understand them to say, "Don't pretend you do not love when you do." There

are those, who feign a love that they do not feel;
but I would not call this love's dissimulation.
It is rather dissimulation from the absence of
love.   But there is a dissimulation which belongs to love itself.   There is a false shame,
which pretends it does not care for the object—
which tempts love to hide itself within the
heart.   Why does Paul say, " I am not *ashamed*
of the Gospel of Christ "?   Because he knew
the tendency of man's heart to be afraid of its
own revealings.   He knew that affection never
likes to display its treasures.   He knew that
love has been taught to deem itself a weakness,
and to blush over its own ecstasy.   Therefore, he
cries, " Oh, ye, who cherish tender sympathies,
hide them not from one another.   Defraud not
your brother of his tribute from your soul.
Conceal not the warmth that is in you; one day
you shall be glad that your heart did not hide
its gold."   So says Paul, and I feel with him.
I feel that the sting of death is never so painful
as when I have kept back part of the price of
love.   My friend is gone, and I did not tell him.
He walked side by side with me, and never
knew.   I had the opportunity, and I have let
it go.   I had the love, and I dissimulated that

love. I pretended I was cold, indifferent, un-
moved. I thought it was a strong thing, a
manly thing, to be made of iron. I suppressed
the overflowings of my spirit; I closed the
gates, and shut them in; and now they come
out in vain. There is nothing so sad to me as a
thought like that. Sometimes we have reflec-
tions as to whether we have used every remedy
for the *body*. Is there any remedy for the body
like love? We call it a spiritual thing; doubtless, but its power is over the physical. Tell
me that someone loves me, and you have given
me a new draught of life—water of life, as our
Lord calls it. How many an early victim would
have been kept alive by a deeper draught of
love! How many a withered rose would have
bloomed; how many a drooping flower would
have revived! A little word by the wayside, the
pressure of a hand, the ring of a voice, the
glance of an eye, the beat of a responsive heart,
would have sweetened the waters of Mara and
revealed the promised land. Hast thou an
alabaster box? break it, oh, my soul. Hide it
not; hoard it not. Wait not to garnish the
sepulchre; pour it on the living head. Give it
to the weary limbs; shed it on the throbbing

brow; shower it on the fainting heart. Thy love was made to shine before the cross; take heed that it linger not behind.

LXXXI.

Liberty in Christ.

Romans vii. 4 v.

"Ye also are become dead to the law by the body of Christ."

LOVE always makes a man dead to law; laws were made for weak love. Why are there criminal courts? Because Cain does not love his brother. If Cain did love his brother, you might abolish all the criminal courts to-morrow. Imagine a message brought to Paul that all the laws against crime had been suspended; would he feel more free to do what was wrong? He would simply be unaffected by the message. He would say: "I have all along been dead to these criminal laws. They have never been a motive to me. It was not on their account that I abstained from hurting my brother. I regret the putting out of the candle for the men who walk in the night; but to me it

extinguishes nothing. It has itself been long
extinguished by the blaze of the sun. It is
no magistrate's hand that has kept my hand
from my brother; it is the grasp of love.
Whenever I would injure my brother's body,
there has floated before my sight another body
—the body of Christ. I have seen in Him
what a grand thing it is to be a man. I have
seen in Him what a beautiful structure this
human frame is. It has become to me a
temple, a place of reverence. I would not put
forth my hand to mar its symmetry. I need
no power to restrain me; I ask no motive to
deter me; I require no commandment to
prohibit me. *Love* is the flaming sword that
keeps the way to the tree of life; I have
become dead to the law."

Oh, Thou Divine Love, whose human form
embodies all my dreams, the tree of life is safe
if I have Thee. I could not violate one leaf
in *Thy* presence. Men are crying out that the
safeguards are being withdrawn. The fires of
hell are less visible than they used to be. Be
it so; the fires of hell were never the flaming
sword of *my* garden. I do not think they
would have kept me from injuring any branch

of the tree; I was always dead to their law.
But when I saw *Thee*, I beheld a more threaten-
ing flame.   It burned in front of my heart.
It would not let me pass to hurt my brother;
it menaced me with a pain compared to which
the old fire was feeble.   Ever so stand, Thou
Son of Man.   Stand in the breach, and protect
my brother by Thy love in me.   Stand in the
scene of my passions and guard the old tree.
Then, though the thunder roll not, though the
lightnings flash not, though the storm has
ceased to be an avenger, though the subter-
ranean fires are almost lost to view, the flame
in my heart shall be an ample barrier to any
deed unkind.   The fetters removed from my
hand shall enclose my spirit; I shall be taken
captive by love when I am loosed from law.

LXXXII.

The Condition of Beholding.

Hebrews xii. 14 v.

"Without holiness no man shall see the Lord."

IT is not a threat; it is a calm statement of the law of beauty. Spiritual beauty can only be seen by its possessor. Outward loveliness can be seen by a deformed body; but spiritual loveliness is invisible to a deformed mind. It would not help you to get into the picture-gallery; it would not help you to put your hand on the canvas; it is not a distance of sight, but of soul. You might stand under the very eye of the portrait and call it a plain face. So did the spectators in the great gallery of New Testament pictures; they admired Barabbas and neglected Jesus. In Barabbas they saw that which was familiar to them; it was in themselves, and therefore they recognised it in him. His was a material beauty—strong, muscular, athletic, the mirror of its age. The age would easily have seen its lord in *him;* but the beauty of Jesus was of another kind.

It was not massive; it was not muscular; it was not majestic; it was not such as we figure in the leaders of armies. It was the beauty of holiness, the beauty of self-restraint, the beauty of the calm sea which hides within its breast the capacity for storm. In such a face they could not see the Lord. It was not their ideal of lordship. It was not in their heart, and, therefore, it could not be in their eye. That which thou seest is the reflection of thyself; that which thou hearest is the echo of thyself; that which thou admirest is the image of thyself. Art thou a worshipper of Barabbas? it is because thou art Barabbas; thou beholdest in him thine own ideal of glory. No man can be attracted to a side of the gallery opposite to his own nature. Not by thy sin but by thy holiness art thou drawn to the face of Jesus. Even where thou comest in the *sense* of sin, it is not sin that brings thee. No man can see Christ's beauty but *by* His beauty. Only love can behold love; only purity can discern purity; only that which is Divine can gaze on the Divine. Not by contrast but by resemblance is a man brought to Jesus. Though *He* stands on the mountain and thou on the plain, it is His own light by which thou seest Him. If thou art attracted towards Him, it can only be by Himself. Therefore, in thy dust and ashes, lift up thy head. There is gold behind the dust; there is fire below the ashes. The vision of His beauty is itself the prodigal's best robe; only by holiness couldst thou have seen His face.

LXXXIII.

The Entrance into the City.

Revelation xxi. 12, 13 v.

"A wall great and high . . . and twelve gates . . . on the east, three gates; on the north, three gates; on the south, three gates; and on the west, three gates."

THE city of God seems here at once to repel and to invite. It has a great and high wall which fences it from the outsider. Yet it has twelve gates of entrance within the wall—as if it had no wish to ward off any one. On which side are we to dwell? Is it hard or is it easy to be a Christian, a member of the city of God? We must look at both aspects;

there is a high wall, but there are twelve gates. There is a barrier of self-sacrifice which separates this city from every other city; and that is the wall. But there is infinite diversity in the sacrifice; and that represents the gates. The men in the city of God have all washed their robes in Christ; but they have not all washed the same robes. Paul and Nathaniel could never have got in by the same gate; each had to sacrifice in his own way. Paul gave up his will with great struggle; he had a strong soul, and the old life died slowly. Nathaniel yielded with little more than a sigh; he was born under the fig tree, and his heart was not capable of storm. Shall their experience be the same? How can it? Within the wall they will tell of separate worlds; Paul shall praise the thorn, and Nathaniel shall extol the fig tree.

I thank Thee, oh, Father, that Thy city has so many gates; I thank Thee that there is such provision for the twelve tribes of man. The holy temple of Thy Christ has doors on every side. Some open on the rugged north, to admit by ways of trouble. Some unbar to the sunny south, to let in by quiet paths. Some have their entrance from the east, to invite by the hope of morning. Some have their opening from the west, to kindle the torch of memory at the light of the setting sun. Not all have sought Thy Christ for one beauty. Some have come in at Bethlehem, attracted by the meeting of earth and heaven. Some have entered at Calvary, drawn by the weight of human sin. Some have found admittance at Olivet, inspired by the vision of immortality. And some have reached Thy temple by way of Samaria; they are captivated by the Christ of human charity, caught by the brotherhood of man with man. Within Thy holy city, within Thy holy temple, these diverse minds shall meet. Outside the gates they have quarrelled, wrangled, denied each his brother's door. But, within, the various colours make one rainbow, and all the gates are gates of gold. Each reveals his own gem; each is enlarged by gazing on another's, till from the blended fragments there is woven Thy crown of light, Thy light that has a place for every ray, the fulness of Him that filleth all in all.

LXXXIV.

The Ripest Communion.

Psalm xxv. 1 v.

"Unto Thee, O Lord, do I lift up my soul."

THERE are three upliftings in the religious life
—hope, faith, and love. Hope is the lifting up
of the eyes; it is the time of youth. There is
always a charm in unfinishedness when we are
young; the unreached land is the desired land.
Faith is the lifting up of the hands; it is the
time of manhood. Every lifting of the man's
hand is a seed sown in faith. He is in all
things a speculator; he trusts to the mercy of
the coming day. Love is the lifting up of the
soul; it is the time of age. I have always felt
that the autumn of life is the season in which
we first view things as they are. Hope and
faith are in the future; love is in the present.
The eye looks forward; the hand stretches onward; but the soul never moves from its place;
it admires here and now. To have the soul
lifted up to God is what men commonly call
death. The Psalmist says we can reach it

without dying, can reach it to-day, this moment,
by one flight of love. Love is the true lifting
of the soul—the true death. It brings me from
time into eternity, from the changeful into the
abiding. It raises me into a world where there
is no future, no to-morrow, no wish to look forward—where the Divine *presence* is fulness of
joy. It makes me independent of memory,
independent of hope, independent of change.
It restores to me the life of the butterfly; it
magnifies the moment; it bids the sun stand
still. It is the end of all climbing, the close
of all longing, the satisfaction of all aspiring,
the goal of all seeking—the rest that remaineth
to the people of God.

Son of Man, lift up my soul. There is no
need to wait for death; death lifts not so high
as love. Love is the swiftest of all flights into
Thy presence. I know why John lay on Thy
bosom; because he had the most rapid wing.
Hope is beautiful, but it cannot rest; it will
not let Peter make a tabernacle for Thee.
Faith is beautiful, but it cannot rest; it bids
Paul press forward for the mark of Thy prize.
But love reposes. It rests on Thy bosom
because it is *Thy* bosom—because it can dream

N

of nothing beyond. The uplifted eye has an expanse before it; the uplifted hand has a work before it; but the uplifted soul basks in Thy present glory. It says Thy will be done. It buries prayer in praise. It loses Thy rainbow in Thy Ararat. It forgets the thought of to-morrow in the rest of to-day. I shall say "*Now* is the accepted time" when Thou hast lifted up my soul.

LXXXV.

The Preparation of Man's Dwelling-Place.

John xiv. 2 v.

" In My Father's house are many mansions . . . I go to prepare a place for you."

WE have here the telescope and the microscope. The one reveals the vast places of the universe —the many mansions of the Father; the other fixes upon a unit in the void, "I go to prepare a place for you." Often have I been startled by the vastness of that sea in which my little life is moving; I seem but a speck amid myriad waves. Yet, it is not the distance that startles

The uplifted soul buries prayer in praise

many mansions of My Father

The telescope reveals vast places of the universe &

The microscope — fixes upon a unit in the void I go to prepare a place for you me. If you could give me wings by which in a moment I could reach the end of the universe, it would not bring me one step nearer rest. I want to know what *is* at the end of the universe. Is there a human soul there? Is there anything that can respond to my spirit? Is there aught that can love when I love, weep when I weep, joy when I joy? Is there a pulse of sympathy that can answer to the pulse of my heart? Is there a place prepared for me? I cannot get that place by going over the bridge; I can only get it by some one going over before me. What I want is a heart already there, a kindred soul to meet me, a human life to greet me. The "going before" is itself the "preparing." I want no gorgeous furniture in my room of the Father's house. I am afraid the furniture may be too gorgeous. I want something homely—like home. I seek an old glance of the eye, an old ring of the voice, an old clasp of the hand. I seek the ancient sympathy that has linked man to man, the earthly love that has knit heart to heart, the human trust that has bound life to life. I seek in eternity the image of time; that is the place I would have prepared for me.

N 2

Let not thy heart be troubled; in the vast spaces there is a home for *thee*. The Son of Man has gone before; there is a region prepared for humanity. There is a spot in this stupendous universe where human nature dwells. That spot is thy one comfort, thy one glory. No other glory would make up for it. There may be golden streets and pearly gates and sapphire thrones. There may be rivers clear as crystal, and trees rich in foliage, and flowers full of bloom. There may be suns that never set, and hands that never weary, and lives that never die. But about these many things thy heart is not troubled. One thing is needful, without which all were vain— the sympathy of a brother's soul. Content mayst thou be to have no revealing of the many lights in the upper chamber, since thou hast been allowed to gaze on one glimmering light of love—"I go to prepare a place for you."

LXXXVI.

God's Work and Man's Work.

Philippians ii. 12, 13 v.

"Work out your own salvation with fear and trembling : for it is God which worketh in you both to will and to do of His good pleasure."

THERE are two parts in every great work—a working in and a working out. The working in is always the Divine part. It is very easy to work out an idea when once you have got it; but the mystery is the getting of it. What is the mystery of the bee-hive? It is not the making of the hive; it is the conceiving of it. If you can tell me how the idea was worked *in*, I will tell you how the plan was worked out. The thing which wakes my wonder is the instinct—the process *within* the bee; I call it God's work. So it is with my soul. I, too, am helping to build a hive — a great home of humanity, named the Kingdom of God. I know not how it is done ; I know not even what part of the building I am aiding to construct; I only know that an impulse of life moves me. That

impulse is God working within me. Whither it
tends I cannot see. The making of the hive
eludes me. I am travelling through the night—
carrying I know not what, to places I know not
where. Only, the impulse says "go," and I do
go; I work out what God works in. I cannot
fathom His designs; He has inspired me to the
work by designs less than His own. He sends
me to chase a butterfly when He means me to
win a kingdom. No matter, I work what I will
not; I compass what I conceive not; I perform
what I plan not. I do what is not in my dream
by the very effort to fulfil it. I seek, like
Abraham, a foreign country, and I find myself
in the land of Canaan.

Son of Man, help me to work out the plan of
Thy salvation. Even though it should be by
lower motives, guide me to build the hive.
Cause me to lay my stores of honey in the right
place—I mean, the right place for *Thee*. Put it
where its sweetness may refresh others, even
though its investment may be a failure to myself.
Fill me with fear and trembling at the solemnity
of my own position. Impress me with the
awfulness of being an unconscious worker for
Thee. Teach me the untold possibilities of my

smallest action. Tell me that the stone which I leave in the desert may be one day the centre of Thy city—not because it has changed its place, but because Thy places have come round it. Let me consecrate by prayer my most common deed ere ever it quits my hand, knowing that Thou hast a motive behind my motive. It shall be cast further than my utmost strength can throw, for it is impelled by a purpose higher than its own.

LXXXVII.

Kindness to Animals.

Genesis i. 26 v.

"And God said, Let us make man in our image, and let them have dominion over the fish of the sea, and over the fowl of the air, and over the cattle."

GOD never gives dominion to any creature which has not reached His image. His image is love. Other things *belong* to God; but God *is* love. No creature that has not love will be allowed to have a permanent empire. The Father of Mercy will not put the reins of government into a hand

Dominion

that has no heart. Dominion is a very solemn thing; it may oppress, crush, destroy. The Father must have a guarantee for its gentleness. What guarantee can there be but His own image —the possession of a nature tender as the Divine? Ye who torture the beast of the field, have you considered the ground of your authority? Have you pondered why it is that God has given you the dominion? It is because He meant you to have His image ere you began to reign. If you have not a tender heart, you have no right to reign; you are a usurper. Is it not written that Christ Himself has authority to exercise judgment because He is the Son of *Man*—because He has a soul of infinite tenderness? Shall the disciple be above his Lord? If you would reign with Him, you must first suffer with Him—feel the pains of sympathy for the wants below. It is the meek who shall inherit the earth; God's dominion is for God's love.

My Father, fill me with love for things beneath me. Forbid that I should be cruel to the beast of the field. Give me the tenderness that is born of reverence. Teach me to revere the creation that is under me. Was not its life a stream from Thy life? Is not its life a mystery to me even now? Does it not accomplish without reasoning what I cannot do *by* reasoning? Let me uncover my head before the mystery. Shall I bruise that which is so full of Thee, which surpasses me even while it obeys me? I think I can understand why men of old worshipped the animal. It was the sense of an avenue of knowledge beyond all human avenues —that there are more modes of Thy inspiration than we dream of in our philosophies. Let me take up tenderly that which I do know. There are wants in beast and bird which to me are no mysteries, for they are my own. Give me fellowship with these, oh, my Father. Extend my philanthropy downward. Let me enter into sympathy with their hunger, their thirst, their weariness, their cold, their frequent homelessness. Let me give their wants a place in my prayers. Let me remember them in the struggles of the forest. Let me remember them in the neglect of the city. Let me remember them in the winter's frost and snow. Let me be to them what Thou hast been to me—a protector, a Providence. I shall be worthy to have Thy dominion when I have reached Thy image.

LXXXVIII.

The Order of Life.

Psalm xxvii. 5, 6 v.

" For in the time of trouble He shall hide me in His
pavilion; He shall set me upon a rock; and now shall
mine head be lifted up above mine enemies round about me."

THERE are three stages in the spiritual life—the
pavilion, the rock, and the mount. It begins in
the secret of the pavilion. The troubles of the
world are at first concealed from it. Life appears
a more radiant thing than it really is. And it
is well it should be so. We would never enter
on the voyage if our first sight were not that
of the summer sea. By-and-by the illusion
vanishes. We come out from the pavilion which
hides the troubles of life. We pass from innocence into struggle. We stand upon a rock—
the symbol of defence, the sign of resisting
strength. It is our age of warfare, of battle, of
temptation. At last comes the final stage—
peace. Our head is lifted above our enemies;
we are raised from the rock to the mountain,
and look down. The struggle is over; the rest

of the pavilion is restored. But it is no longer the rest of innocence. It is the calm of temptation conquered, the peace of sorrow vanquished, the silence of warfare passed. The quiet of age is better than the quiet of youth. Youth can hide me from my enemies; but age can lift me above my enemies.

Oh, my Father, lead me through this path of Thine. Give me Thy pavilion in life's morning. Hide from my opening eye the storms of this world. Let me start with a vision of its beauty alone. And yet, I would not always dwell within Thy hiding-place. Bring me in time from the pavilion to the rock. I would know life as it *is*, by-and-by. I would meet its clouds; I would brave its storms; I would breast its billows. I would not have men say, " It was easy for *him* to live; he was hid all his life within a pavilion." When I have seen the world in rose-colours for a little while, I would stand upon a rock and buffet the waves. But neither would I end here, oh, my Father. I know that there is a last state resembling the first. There is a haven where men repose, not by hiding, but by conquering. Lead me to that rest. It is not the rose-coloured rest of the pavilion; but it is better. It admits other colours than the rose; it brings in the whole rainbow. It vindicates the seared and yellow leaf. It tells me that youth is not the only fire that can kindle the flower. It tells me that there is a peace passing knowledge that can come *through* knowledge. Thy dove on the banks of Jordan is beautiful; but the angels that minister to the wilderness are more beautiful still. Lead me to the rest that lies beyond the rock. When Thou hast lifted up my head above my enemies, I shall not need the secret of Thy pavilion.

LXXXIX.

Reverence for the Past.

2 Corinthians iv. 12 v.

"Death worketh in us, but life in you."

I UNDERSTAND the words to depict an old man speaking to the new generation. He says :—
"I have had the nut to crack; you will get the kernel. I have had the labour; you will have the joy. I have had the toil of making the

fortune; you will have the ease of spending it."
It is a wonderfully true picture of the beginning
and ending of things. The beginning of every
new life is hard on its possessor. The first man
of science is treated as a wizard; the first social
reformer is called a revolutionary; the first poet
is deemed mad. How many things were forbidden to our fathers which to us are the breath
of common air, and as easy as its breathing!
Christ is one of these. To be a Christian was,
in Paul's days, to be a weakling. It was a thing
to be ashamed of; it was not the fashion. But
Paul says a time is coming when it shall be the
fashion, when it shall be counted a shame to be
anything else. He says:—" Let the younger
generation know that what I sow they shall
reap. Let them know that there is a day
approaching when Christ shall be an atmosphere.
Let them learn that the precepts of the mount
shall ere long be the precepts of the plain. Let
them remember that the things which I speak
in whispers shall be uttered aloud—taught in
the schools, proclaimed in the temples, demanded in the market-place, desired in the
haunts of pleasure, expected in the hearth
and home. My strait gate shall be their

broadway; my shadow their light; my weakness their strength; my straining their strain of music. Death worketh in me, but life in them.

My soul, art thou looking with contempt on the dead past? It deserves a monument from thee. Hast thou forgotten that the sun in which thou baskest had its rising in blood? Hast thou forgotten that thy life was death to somebody? Hast thou forgotten that thy privileges were the pain of thy fathers? Art thou contrasting thy breadth with the narrowness of the ancients? If they had not been narrow, thou wouldst not have been broad. When Herod is seeking the young child to kill it, what can men do but guard it? There is a time in which faith ought to lie in swaddling bands. In its infancy it is helpless, speechless; and it is in the midst of foes. Ought it not to be protected, isolated, fenced round and round? Yes; and the men who did so should be honoured. It could never have said, "All power is given unto Me in heaven and on earth," if it had not begun with the bands of Bethlehem. Thou that art in the enjoyment of liberal things, build a monument to the narrowness of thy

My privileges were the pain of thy fathers —

fathers. Life works in thee because death worked in them.

XC.

Retrospect and Forecast.

1 Corinthians xi. 24, 26 v.

"This do in remembrance of Me." " Ye do show the Lord's death till He come."

WHAT is the motive assigned for keeping this feast? Is it something in the past or something in the future? It is both; the avenue is lighted at each of the gates. There is an illumination of the past, "This do in remembrance of Me"; and there is an illumination of the future, "Ye do show the Lord's death till He come." Do you deem it strange that the mind should be drawn by two such opposite motives? Is it not ever so with our memorials of the departed? When you go to put flowers upon a grave, what is the motive that prompts you?—to keep memory green? Doubtless; but is that all? Why do you wish to keep memory green? It is

[handwritten margin note, left: The Lord's Supper for what purpose?]

[handwritten margin note, right: Two opposite motives. looking forward and backward?]

Pleasures of memory

because you are looking forward as well as backward. You are convinced the old days will come again. If it were not for that hope, you could not plant your flower; you would rather let memory wither. Some have written of the pleasures of memory, and some of the pleasures of hope. But has it occurred to either that the pleasures of memory *are* the pleasures of hope? Has it occurred to either that these are twin sisters, who cannot live apart? When hope dies, memory cries out to be killed; she cannot abide alone. When memory goes with her flowers to the grave, hope calls from the shadowy land, "Occupy till I come." If she did not hear that call, she could not plant her flower. My Lord tells me that when I build to His past I am prompted by His future. It is the light of Easter morn that leads me to the sepulchre; it is the gleam of resurrection that conducts me to the broken body, "As often as ye eat this bread, ye do show the Lord's death till He come."

Therefore, my soul, be strong. When there comes over thee the impulse to keep thy memory green, remember it is from life, not death, that the impulse comes. Memory may plant the flower, but hope selects it. No tribute of thy heart was ever paid to the dead; that which thou lovest is to thee always alive. It may seem an act of pure remembrance; but its mainspring is not remembrance. Its mainspring is the belief that the days will come back again. It is not the broken body that thou seest; it is the body unbroken once more. It is not the cross thou beholdest; it is the cross superseded. It is not the grave-clothes on which thou gazest; it is the grave-clothes bound in a napkin. It is not the stone on the sepulchre thou markest; it is the angel sitting on the stone. Thy voluntary remembrance is an unconscious prophecy; thy night is seen by the coming day.

XCI.

The Thought for the Act.

1 Kings viii. 18, 19 v.

"And the Lord said unto David, Whereas it was in thine heart to build an house unto My name, thou didst well that it was in thine heart: nevertheless thou shalt not build the house."

A MOST remarkable passage. David wants to build a temple to the Lord. God will not let him; He desires it to be reserved for other hands. But He tells him that by reason of the very thought he is counted one of God's builders. David's temple was never in stone and lime. It stood on no actual ground; it filled no visible space. It was only a cathedral in the heart. Its walls were in the imagination; its arches were in the fancy; its pillars were in the mind; its altars were in the soul. Yet God says that this cathedral of the heart shall be accepted as a real edifice. He says that this shadowy structure, this air-castle, this product of unfulfilled design, shall have the value of a house in stone and

[margin notes: David desire to build a temple unto God's name; David one of God's builders; The cathedral of the heart]

lime. It shall have a price put upon it in heaven equal to any finished building. The architecture of the city of God is not limited to houses made with hands. There are whole streets within it which never existed outwardly. There are temples which men meant to raise. There are hospitals which philanthropy intended to found. There are schools which benevolence planned to institute. The structures that God accepts are, for the most part, like Jacob's ladder—built in a dream. We raise palaces in our hearts, when our hands can only erect mud dwellings; but God keeps His eye on the palaces not begun, and attributes not to us the finished tenements of clay. He measures my workmanship by the edifice in my soul.

Father, I have no temple built which is worthy of Thee. There is nothing which my hands have reared that I would be willing to live by. Whenever I make Thee a cathedral, there rises up in my imagination another house which puts it to shame. Take that other house, oh, my Father. It is untouched by hammer, or axe, or chisel; it has as yet neither a local habitation nor a name. It is all in the spirit; it is what I *mean* to do.

Cathedral in my imagination

o 2

But Thou art the Father of spirits. The topmost towers in Thy city are towers of intention. My performance has never come up to my thought. Solomon built Thee a house, and David planned it; but David's was a grander house than Solomon's. My hand can but feebly represent the movements of my soul. Thou seest the " Paradise Lost " in the heart of Milton, and it is more beautiful than the one in the book. The temple in my heart is Thy house not made with hands. It is my true Babel; it reaches unto heaven; its spire touches the sky. It is Thy New Jerusalem; come and dwell therein; walk round about it; mark its bulwarks; consider its towers, and let the river of its pleasures glad Thee. Thou canst not be gladdened by what I *do;* but the river of Thy pleasures is the aspiring of my heart.

XCII.

The Comfort of Christ's Experience.

John xvi. 33 v.

"In the world ye shall have tribulation; but be of good cheer, I have overcome the world."

Christ spoke these words at a time when to all appearance the world had overcome *Him*. He was standing on the borders of death. There *were* times in His life in which we could have understood such an utterance. We could have understood it in the moment of resurrection, when He had *beaten down* His calamities. We could have understood it in the moment of ascension, when He had left His calamities behind. But to say it in the very midst of His calamities— that seems a strange thing. And yet, why so? When does a man overcome his enemy? Is it when he beats him down? Hardly; that is to conquer the enemy, but not the enmity. Is it when he leaves him behind and soars into other spheres? Nay; that is to escape rather than to overcome. The real hour of overcoming your enemy is the hour in which you find some good in him—the hour in which you stand in his presence, and are not consumed. So was it with Jesus and the trials of this life. He beat them down in His rising; He escaped them in His ascending; but only in His voluntary Cross did He overcome them. His moment of world-conquest was the moment in which He took the cup. When He tasted that cup and found it not to be absolutely bitter—that was the hour in which He truly overcame.

Son of Man, it is Thy voice on the *Cross* that brings me good cheer. Thou hast other voices of triumph; but they have no bearing on me. I cannot *beat down* my calamities; Thy resurrection is beyond me. I cannot escape my calamities; Thy ascension surpasses me. But I can take Thy cup, for it is my own cup. It is a cup without mystery and without miracle—made up of my own sorrows. And when I see it in Thy hand, and hear Thee say, "I have tasted it unharmed," my heart grows light within me. If Thou hast found rest to Thy soul after taking the yoke, I may well be of good cheer; I can take courage when I learn of *Thee*. I have heard betimes a bather call to his comrades on the shore, "Come in; it is not cold." So is it with

Thee. Thy voice comes to me from the waves of trouble—waves in which, one day, I myself must plunge. It cries: "Don't be afraid; I have tested the waters; they are not so cold after all, nor so stormy. Though they rise up to the brim, they will not overflow thee. I have met them at their fulness; I know the utmost they can do. And I tell you that their utmost is not overwhelming. I have measured their bounds and retained my courage; I have received their force and kept my footing; I have learned their violence and held fast my faith; I have sounded their depths, and there is land below. "Be of good cheer, I have overcome the world."

Hear God's voice from the waves of Trouble

XCIII.

The World's Salutation to Christianity.

Philippians iv. 22 v.

" All the saints salute you, chiefly they that are of Cæsar's household."

THE greenest wreath of welcome to Christ is sent from the pit of the theatre. Cæsar's household! —that is the last place from which we should have expected the first note of greeting. Rome was the most worldly spot on earth. Cæsar's palace was the worst spot in Rome. Cæsar's household was the worst spot in the palace. Why did not the wreath come from the upper lives ? We should not have wondered if it had been sent by the men of the desert—by those who had shaken the dust of this world from their feet, and were waiting for another. But Cæsar's household was the home of the most crowded humanity. It was the place where the lowest ranks met and jostled each other. We can understand the rapturous greeting of the Christ by one like the prophetess Anna, who had lived all her life in solitude and

" departed not from the temple night and day."
But, amid this motley mass, amid this surging
crowd, amid this turgid stream of human
passions, where was there room to see Christ's
beauty? Is not Christ's beauty the power
of sacrifice — the strength of self - denial?
Why was it not first seen by the hermit?
Wherefore did its earliest wreath come from
Cæsar's household?

It is because there is no self-denial like that
of the thoroughfare. Thou who art flying from
the world in search of a sacrifice of self, thou art
flying from the very thing thou seekest. There are
two kinds of self-denial. There is a self-denial
which exists in separation from the world; it is
the sacrifice of giving up, and doubtless it has its
pain. But there is another and a more arduous
self-denial—that which consists in taking on.
There is a sacrifice which only comes by *union*
with the world; thou shalt find it in the meeting
with thy brother man. It is a much easier thing
for thee to give up than to take on. To throw
away sympathy with thine own past may be
something; but to enter into sympathy with *my*
past is more. To cast off thine old garment may
be sad; but to put on *my* garment requires more

courage still. It is only in Cæsar's household
that such a task is possible. Thou canst disrobe
thyself in the desert; but the city demands that
thou shalt put on thy brother's robe. It is
where man meets man that thy sacrifice begins.
It is easy to feel thy nothingness in the presence
of the mountains and the stars; it is a light
thing to be humble before *God*. But to yield
thyself to a frail mortal, to sink thyself in the
interest of a fellow-sinner, to merge thyself in
sympathy with a creature of the dust—this puts
the hermit's life to shame, this is the flower of
sacrifice. Truly, I wonder not that, amid all the
wreaths of welcome, Christ's sweetest salutation
came from Cæsar's household.

XCIV.

The Approach of Nicodemus.

John iii. 2 v.

"The same came to Jesus by night."

To come by night is not a universal experience. There are, in truth, all times for coming to Christ. The radiant morn of hope, the meridian strength of manhood, the burden and the heat of life's afternoon, the twilight of disappointed joy—all these are both times and reasons for our coming. But night seems a reason for not coming; it is the coming in darkness, in doubt, in intellectual depression. We do not so much wonder at shadows *following* the coming. It is the property of light to make shadows. The darkness of a Thomas grows out of his love, and the fear lest it should be vain. But to come *in* shadow, to come when love itself is in its infancy, to come when every motive prompts to stay—this appears a very arduous thing. The doubt of Nicodemus was more discouraging than the doubt of Thomas. Thomas had a background in memory; the darkness of the moment was painted on the

Nicodemus

Doubt of Nicodemus

There are in truth all times for coming to christ.

Thomas

Doubt of thomas

canvas of a bright past. But Nicodemus had no Christian memories to support him. He *began* in the night; it was his first experience. He had never seen the morning star, never heard the lark's note, never known how the world could be kindled by the day. He was called while yet under the shadow; he came by night.

Son of Man, I am glad that Thou hast suffered him thus to come. I am glad that, amid the many approaches to Thee, there is one for a life so poor. I am glad there is a stage below the coming of a little child. The child comes in emptiness. But night is worse than empty; it is a space filled with spectres. I thank Thee that Thou hast admitted into Thy kingdom a man from such a home. He saw nothing about Thee but Thy works. Thy beauty was veiled to him. He had not even seen that youth can be renewed—that a man may be born again when he is old. Yet, in his rags, Thou hast taken him in. He asked only to work with Thee—to do that kind of labour which he saw Christians do. He would sign no creed, he would make no confession, he would join no church; he asked but to be a helper of humanity; and Thou saidst, "Come." He had a back-door to Thy communion table; but he sat down with the best. He never saw Thee on the mount; but he was privileged to meet Thee in the vale; he took up Thy crucified body. Such is ever Thy work for those who come by night. Thou leadest them by the paths of the human; Thou makest them the ministers to man. They do not always take Thy name; those who wrestle for daybreak are afraid to take a name; they would bless and pass by. But Thou givest them the name they have not assumed; Thou callest them after Thyself. They have come to Thee in the night; but they shall claim their brotherhood with the children of the day.

XCV.

The Later Glory.

Acts ii. 17, 19 v.

"And it shall come to pass in the last days, saith God . . . I will show wonders in heaven above, and signs in the earth beneath."

"In the last days." I always thought wonder belonged to the first days—the days of our youth. I thought it was a mark of ignorance, a sign of immaturity. Is not the great fear of our time just the fear that wonder will be killed by knowledge? We are afraid that, as we learn, we shall cease to admire, and that we shall see less of God the more we know of man. But here, the wonder comes at the end, not at the beginning; it belongs to the last days. I am told to look upon the sense of mystery, not as something that fades with the past, but as something that dawns with the future. I am told to view it, not as a feeling which knowledge shall explode, but as a sentiment which knowledge shall foster. I am told to think of it, not as the product of ignorance, but as a thing which

ignorance has retarded and which perfect science
will reveal. I used to think the stones of my
temple had fallen from heaven. But now I have
found the quarry from which they were taken;
and, behold, it is on earth. What then? Shall
my wonder die? Nay; rather, it ought to be
for the first time born. There is no wonder
where there is no workmanship. To fall from
heaven is less marvellous than to grow from
earth. My temple has not come down ready-
made; but it has been made in a manner more
wonderful still. It has risen through the efforts
of myriad souls—each laying a separate stone,
each unconscious what or where he laid. Each
comes to build for his own end; and, lo, at the
close, there is one harmonious structure, offering
room to all. This *shall* be, this ought to be,
the wonder of the Lord.

My soul, why art thou ever sighing for
the former days? Why hast thou placed thy
paradise ever in the past? Thy paradise is not
in the past; it is on before. Thou hast built
many a monument to thy vanished youth. Hast
thou never built a monument to thy coming
age? Why has thy wonderland been always in
the olden time? God would place thy wonder-

land, not in the first, but in the last days. His gates of gold for thee open in the west. Men speak of aspiring youth; God speaks of aspiring age. The birds of His highest heaven twitter in the *evening* air. Faith's song is more wonderful at the setting than at the rising of the sun. Love's voice is more prophetic when it has learned the labours of the wing. Hope's trill is more melodious when it issues from the cloud. Joy's note is more assuring when it comes from the closing day. The old man's dreams are better than the young man's visions; truly, thy Father has kept His best wine until the last.

THE END.

Printed by Cassell & Company, Limited, La Belle Sauvage, London, E.C.
20.195

CPSIA information can be obtained
at www.ICGtesting.com
Printed in the USA
LVHW100952221220
674870LV00028B/242